Praise for
Engagement, Retention & Growth

This book provides a sumptuous feast of practical ideas for leaders who want to navigate their organization into prosperity and success. Even though we can't control when or how fast the economy pulls out of the doldrums, leaders can inject vitality into their organization by following this advice.

> —JACK ZENGER, CEO of Zenger Folkman, best-selling co-author of *How To Be Exceptional: Drive Leadership Success by Magnifying Your Strengths*

ENGAGEMENT RETENTION & GROWTH

10 Strategic Solutions for Sustainable Corporate Expansion & Employee Retention

Edited by TIGERS Success Series

Strategies presented by

Dianne Crampton • Tony Lacertosa • Michael Bouton • Pamela Brooks • Andrea Adams-Miller
Klaus Kokott• Debra Zimmer • Dan Berryman • Judith Hurlburt • Ida Shessel

Three Creeks
Publishing

Three Creeks Publishing
www.engagement-retention-grown.com
© 2012 by Three Creeks Publishing
Edited by TIGERS Success Series
All rights reserved. Published 2012
Printed in the United States of America

ISBN: 9780984508297
Library of Congress Control Number: 2012945342

Bulk order discounts are available.
Three Creeks Publishing
19464 Summerwalk Place
Bend, OR 97702

DEDICATION

This book is dedicated to every business owner, manager, CEO, consultant and leader who strives for cooperation and collaboration in the workplace. This is the type of workplace that employees enjoy coming to every Monday morning. This is a place where challenges are met head-on with transparency and empowerment.

Here's to all the workforce champions who lead one another through the maze of changing times.

ACKNOWLEDGEMENTS

We are grateful for the collaborative efforts of Dianne Crampton, Tony Lacertosa, Michael Bouton, Pamela Brooks, Andrea Adams-Miller, Klaus Kokott and his partner Richard Wood, Debra Zimmer, Dan Berryman, Judith Hurlburt, Ida Shessel, Pamela McGrew, Sherman Morrison, Heidi Sutherliln, Jeune Taylor, Ted Nelsen, Kathleen Berryman and all the champions in our lives who have influenced us to strive for excellence and to do the right thing.

CONTENTS

Introduction

by TIGERS Success Series

**Thriving in the Wake of the Great Recession:
The Challenges Ahead**

As nations emerge from one of the longest recessions in recent history, leaders are finding themselves wading through uncharted waters. The newly emerging economy is experiencing slower than usual growth, high unemployment, a struggling global economy and strapped financial options to boost capital expenditures.

If History Repeats Itself…

As U.S. businesses move beyond the recession, some will show success while others will fail, be split up, sold off or taken over. If history repeats itself, certain business strategies applied during the recession will determine to a large degree a company's fate.

The Harvard Business Review (HBR) conducted a yearlong study and analyzed the strategy selection and performance of corporate America during the past three global recessions. With three recessions over the past 30 years to collect data from, the 1980 crisis (1980 to 1982), the 1990 slowdown (1990 to 1991), and the 2000 bust (2000 to 2002), HBR revealed some startling findings.

Painfully Slow Recoveries

HBR analyzed strategies of 4,700 public companies, breaking down the data into three periods: the three years before a recession, the three years after, and the recession years. HBR consistently found that 17 percent of the companies in the study didn't survive a recession: They went bankrupt, were acquired, or spun off. The survivors were slow to recover from the battering as well. As a matter of fact, about 80 percent had not regained their pre-recession growth rates for sales and profits three years after a recession ended.

As businesses emerge from the latest recession that began in 2007, what significant challenges will they face? Based on the information gathered from previous recessions, many organizations used strategies such as deep cutbacks and massive layoffs with very little reinvestment back into the company. Now these businesses must contend with this if they are to thrive. Here are some of the challenges businesses, large and small, now face:

1. **Business Infidelity**—Customers, employees, partners, and vendors can be fickle when there is a lack of connection or commitment within an organization. When stakeholders reach this level of disconnect, a business is vulnerable to losing stakeholders to competitors with a better match for stakeholders' needs.

2. **Social Media Soapbox**—In today's social society where customers, the workforce, and prospective employees have instant access to a social media megaphone; leaders are struggling to control their corporate image. They fear, for example, that public comments by disgruntled employees could be picked up by the press. Social media is also a new concept to many business leaders. They are learning that restraining employee engagement with social media isn't the answer. One question is, "How do you let employees loose to participate in social media without sabotaging marketing and public relation efforts?" Another question is, "Can social media actually enhance image through new marketing and public relation efforts?"

3. **Communication Malfunctions**—Snap judgments lead employees to premature conclusions that often result in diminished trust and respect. Other communication failures include poor meeting management so solving problems collectively becomes a problem. When communication is poor, procedures become confused leading to misunderstandings and conflict. Referred to as the *storming phase* of team dynamics, some teams never make it out of this phase. This produces stress. Too much workforce stress results in civility breakdown. Talented employees have other options than to work in an uncivil workplace. This leads to retention issues, which keeps some human resource managers awake a night.

4. **Mismanaged Human Performance**—It is staggering to read recent research on what it costs a company when top performers terminate their employment. There are ranges from 1.5 times the employee's salary up to $7,000 a day *for each day a top performer is missing.* Because of cutbacks,

employee performance, team performance, and responding with empathy to employee recession-related *life crises* have not been priorities in some organizations. Yet it is hard to roar out of the recession and grow when mismanaged human performance results in employees jumping ship.

5. **"Hiring to Fill" Quick Fix**—As companies begin to experience growth, leaders need to fill new positions. The question is how to fill these positions with the right people? Hiring to fill a position can result in a bad and costly hire if the culture of the company and the values of new employees do not align.

6. **Not Recognizing that Every Employee is a Salesperson**— There is a simple business formula: No sales = No profits = No money = No business. The ability to learn and then teach the art of handling objections may literally double or triple profits within a year.

7. **Can't Regroup Fast Enough to Retain Valuable Employees**— The first challenge when initiating change is to capture the emotional commitment of key leaders. The second is to engage employees to champion change. Surviving a recession that has lasted five years or more depends on whether leaders are able to regroup in time without losing talented employees and market share to more agile and progressive competitors.

8. **Lack of Strategies for Unexpected Changes**—The best designed projects, objectives and role assignments can be derailed by personal or external change. Unexpected change is a part of life and creates less impact on a company when strategies are in place to address them.

The experts who collaborate in *Engagement, Retention and Growth* address each of these issues and offer actionable solutions. At TIGERS Success Series we acknowledge that each organization's human characteristics and business needs are distinct. Just as the fur pattern on the face of a tiger or a human fingerprint is unique, so is each workforce. Therefore, the solutions that assist you in roaring out of the recession require customized focus and action planning. It is our hope that the key solutions we are handing you unlock viable solutions for your engagement, retention and growth opportunities.

DIANNE CRAMPTON

About the Author

Dianne Crampton, M. A. helps committed leaders build cooperative work environments and teams of committed and engaged employees.

She accomplishes this using her proprietary TIGERS® team culture process, which stands for trust, interdependence, genuineness, empathy, risk and success. TIGERS® serves merging organizations, organizations undergoing culture change and founding leadership teams with the commitment to be recognized as one of the best companies to work for.

One of the tools she developed for catalyzing change and improving team dynamics earned a nomination by Merrill Lynch for Inc. Magazine's Entrepreneur of the Year Awards. She certifies and licenses human resource professionals in the use of these tools.

A thought leader in the team culture movement, Dianne's work has been published by Berrett-Koehler, Pfeiffer and Three Creeks Publishing. An educator at heart, she has served Costco, Boeing, AT&T, Northrop Grumman and many others for over 23 years.

More information about TIGERS® Success Series is available on page 152.

How to Engage Employees to Champion Change

by Dianne Crampton

Erica Jung, author of *Fear of Flying*, writes, "I have accepted fear as part of life—specifically the fear of change… I have gone ahead despite the pounding in the heart that says: turn back…."

As we know, people often resist change. In my discussion, I am going to talk about how to engage employees to champion change. I will also discuss how to catalyze employees to overcome their natural resistance to these efforts so that desired change is successfully achieved remarkably fast.

I will share the following:

- The components of a catalytic change process where commitment and engagement are desired outcomes.
- How to develop a common understanding of the behaviors required to achieve cooperation during and after change execution.
- Why stories that surface during the change effort build momentum, sustain commitment and drive results remarkably fast.

My goal is to give you actionable ideas. Some of these ideas will raise more questions, such as the following: How do you fill leadership positions with the right people whose natural strengths will prompt employee engagement to champion change? How do you transform a work environment that has become uncivil during the recession? How do you build new internal and external relationships that improve sales and accelerate growth in ways that are cost effective?

The seasoned consultants and coaches with whom I collaborate in *Engagement, Retention and Growth* answer these questions. From my experience as a change agent and team culture consultant, change is like a multi-faceted diamond. No organization goes into change with the same set of initiatives. Each presents a different facet to explore. But there is a common theme. When people move past their natural inclination to resist change, they can then explore new opportunities.

Why Do People Resist Change?

Basically, people like safety and stability. They thrive when basic needs are satisfied, such as food, clothing and shelter. They excel when they belong to a family or group that accepts and supports them. And they like to know that what they do makes a difference and is appreciated.

Social and industrial psychologists study these issues related to human safety and security. Abraham Maslow is known as the father of humanistic psychology. He developed the Hierarchy of Human Needs in a work published in 1954 known as *Motivation and Personality*. His argument is that people have physical and psychological needs that are ingrained motivations. These motivations are focused on survival, safety, belonging, esteem and self mastery.

According to Maslow, once safety and security are satisfied, people are then able to contribute to group efforts, to society and the goals for which these groups strive.

Therefore, it is not surprising that changing from what is known and appears stable is upsetting for many people. If these people are your senior executives, mid managers and employees, the upset is often expressed as resistance and explains why out of every 100 change efforts, more than 66 fail. People do not champion what they resist.

Researchers with the Harvard Business Review (HBR) studied past United States recessions. They especially focused on the recession that occurred in the late 1980s and early 1990s. The goal was to identify what type of business survived these recessions.

They also wanted to know if the organizations that thrived had common characteristics. If so, they could then predict what type of organization would hold its own and successfully weather the current recession that started in 2007.

In the article, *Roaring out of the Recession* published in 2010, HBR reported that historically only 9% of companies emerge from recessions stronger than they were when the recession started. The organizations that succeed in spite of economic downturns have a formula for success. Businesses that fail, however, merely ride on the coat tails of a robust economy until that economy falters. Leaders who do not "shift gears" to climb out of deep recessions when times are bad often take the position that negative economic conditions are out of their control. Nothing could be further from the truth.

The five common characteristics of successful organizations that are in the 9% that recover well are:

- Leaders were transparent and took care in how they downsized to cut costs. Some did not eliminate positions. They cut hours or worked with solutions that employees generated.
- Leaders invested more than their rivals on marketing, assets and research and development.
- They invested in refining systems to operate more efficiently or improve production capabilities.
- Boards of Directors with the foresight to place excellent leaders in the right seats during downturns demanded high levels of leadership

communication which, included vision, coaching, planning, problem solving and system reporting.

- Employees were empowered to champion change by solving problems that affected their immediate scope of work.

A favorite book of mine that addresses the simple and complex parts of ourselves that resist change is *Who Moved My Cheese?* by Spencer Johnson. It is based on the behaviors of four imaginary characters—two mice and two little people.

Sniff is a mouse who sniffs out change early. Scurry is a mouse that scurries into action. Hem is a little person who denies change is happening and then resists it because he is afraid that change will be worse than the status quo. Haw is a little person who adapts to change because he can envision that change will lead to something better.

It is the Hems in organizations that will resist change and sabotage efforts unless leaders are able to convert them into Haws. The way to do this is by effectively communicating a new vision that instills hope. It is showing people that change will lead to something better.

Some of you may have already sniffed that change is looming on the horizon for your organization. Maybe you know that your company will be growing by purchasing other companies, which will cause culture and staffing changes. Maybe you have a hunch that your company will be sold, merged or will lose or gain employees. Maybe you know that your systems need refining. Maybe you are growing and do not have systems in place to manage growth. Maybe there are kinks in your production lines. Maybe you need new equipment and training on how to operate it. Maybe your work environment has lost its civility and is losing key talent. Maybe you just have a gut feeling that you will be required to lead the charge and are searching for resources and information now.

Some of you realize you are working with senior executives and mid managers that are like Hem. You already see them blaming others for failure as they hold on tight to their operations. Maybe you are on the receiving end of their micro managing. Maybe political posturing is increasing. Maybe you are a corporate director being drawn into daily operations by concerned staff.

Regardless of the change dynamics that are surfacing, one thing is certain. When people are committed and engaged in change for the better they scurry into action, sniff out opportunity and make it happen. The key is catalyzing employees with understanding and vision so they are involved in the process and feel that they have some control rather than change being imposed upon them.

Catalyzing Change

I want to now identify for you the components of a catalytic change process where commitment and engagement are key outcomes.

The first step is to understand what catalysis is and why it is important to change. Catalysis is the acceleration of a process. It is an event that sparks something into action. This event creates reactions that take place more effectively or under milder conditions than would otherwise be possible.

In my work with mergers and culture change where team development and cooperation were desired outcomes, I discovered that commitment and engagement required a catalyst that was emotionally intelligent. This is because commitment and engagement are *emotions* that result from something people want that gives them more pleasure than pain and makes sense to them. I learned that unless resistance is addressed head on, change occurs slowly.

A catalytic change event needs to inspire vision and harness imagination. It must create a safe environment for employees to address resistance. It needs to enhance cooperative group processes by improving working relationships while minimizing uncertainty.

We achieve this by catalyzing employees to champion change using five components. For your first take away, these five components are as follows:

- A process for defining behaviors that build cooperation. In this step, all employees contribute their insights. In large organizations this is usually accomplished by a survey and then reporting the results back to the employees. I will share more about the behaviors that build cooperation in your next take away.

- A way to monitor the effectiveness of the group's process. This includes a plan for communicating needs and progress during the change effort. It also includes problem solving, decision-making, meeting management, action planning, plan implementation and conflict resolution. For leaders, it can be as simple as talking regularly with your employees to see what is working and what is not. If employees are encountering unforeseen problems or obstacles during change, use your authority to resolve these issues immediately. Help your employees experience success. They are the front line that drives results.

- An empowerment-based Action Plan that includes insights from employees. This process usually starts at the management level but is refined by bottom-up insights and employee suggestions.

- A process for monitoring change milestones and reporting the results.

- A process for recognizing teams that cooperate with one another and teams that achieve success milestones so that employees experience early successes. It is important for people to understand how to win and what winning looks like during the change effort. This is accomplished through recognition and new stories. I will expand on this for your third take away.

I have streamlined these five components into a hands-on problem solving activity and series of decision-making and action planning facilitations. The hands-on problem solving activity teaches the behaviors that build cooperation in a fun and non-threatening way. This gives employees a common language and understanding of group dynamics that improve relationships and reduce conflict so goals are achieved through more cooperation and support. When the planning team achieves consensus on the behaviors that are most important during the change effort, these become the group's ground rules.

The final step is empowering employees to include their suggestions into the ground rules and developing action plans to which employees also give their input. This employee-empowered fine-tuning produces commitment and accountability for results.

This catalytic process results in a common and company-wide understanding of the behaviors required to enhance cooperation during and after change execution. The bonus is that the organization's culture naturally becomes more cooperative. As long as cooperation continues to be important for rewards and recognition, it will be sustained and occur remarkably fast.

Catalyzing employees to champion change must empower employees to define the safety parameters of group processes. Change must be monitored. How people work together must be cooperative. It is also necessary to facilitate a common understanding of the behaviors that reduce conflict, improve success and recognize team efforts for achieving change milestones.

Let me give you an example of this. I was a consultant to a company that acquired a competitor that produced the same goods and services. There was considerable competition between the two companies. Senior leaders and a number of managers from the acquired company were let go. Their surviving staff was angry and fearful that they would be fired next. Productivity was at a standstill.

After our initial staff interviews and team discoveries, we took the leadership team through the hands-on problem solving activity to learn about the behaviors required to build a new, cooperation-based company.

We successfully catalyzed the employees into envisioning how the new company would be better than either of the previous companies. We helped them identify the behaviors they believed would support and grow the new company and we gave the management team a way to solicit additional ideas from the employees.

The major points of resistance included the grief over leaders who were let go. There was guilt on the part of the remaining leaders that the firing had not been handled well. Then there was fear on the part of other employees of being the next to go. Through consensus facilitation, we empowered the employees to invent a process to let both of the old companies go, to honor past leaders and to move on.

The team decided to bury the hatchet. This was a real hatchet they put into a small coffin, dug a hole on company grounds, prepared eulogies, buried it, and then designed and built a contemplative sitting area with a fountain over it. They memorialized it. They told stories about it. They gave themselves permission to grieve. They created a space where reflection and remembering was okay. Then they got to work building the new company through action plans to which everyone was committed. What was once at a standstill, plugged by grief, anger and resentment gave way gently in an emotionally intelligent way remarkably fast.

This was an extreme case that was costing the organization a few hundred thousands dollars a month in lost revenue. In most catalyzed change situations, identifying the resistance and tackling it head on does not result in such cathartic events. But if handled skillfully, resistance will melt away because people feel safe and are inspired by new hope. The result is that tremendous energy and creativity are released to champion change.

Behaviors That Build Cooperation to Champion Change

For your second take away—what are the behaviors that build cooperation so that employees are naturally engaged to champion change?

During the last recession in the late 1980s and early 1990s, I wanted to know what is necessary to build an ethical, quality-focused, cooperative and successful group of people. This question was the focus of my advanced degree in leadership from Gonzaga University. I reviewed all the group dynamic research I could find in Education, Psychology and Business. Out of these studies emerged six principles or universal values that apply to any group of people regardless of their nationality, ethnic background, gender or age. These principles are trust, interdependence, genuineness, empathy, risk and success. They form the acronym, TIGERS®. When these principles are demonstrated by behaviors that are readily visible in how people treat one another and through the governance of the organization, there are predictable outcomes.

One of the outcomes is that when people cooperate, more is accomplished because there is more pleasure in working on challenging projects together than painful conflict. This happens when working relationships are trustworthy and demonstrated by behaviors that build trust. They are interdependent and rely on the diverse strengths people use to achieve results. If relationships are genuine, people do not feel tricked, manipulated, coerced or lied to. If they are empathetic, people suspend judgment of one another in order to understand each other better. The result is positive inquiry. The benefit is reduced conflict and more cooperation and the desire to strive for collaborative conflict resolution. People are more considerate of others. They are also risk resolving. This means they work to solve problems by bringing diverse perspectives to the table. Planning produces accountability. It is understood that mistakes happen. When they do, the mistakes are analyzed down to the root cause so problems are resolved. When goals are achieved and success is experienced, people feel personally satisfied with the results. Teams celebrate successes and people who cooperated beyond the call of duty to help others achieve success are recognized as well.

The second benefit of understanding the behaviors that build cooperation is engagement and accountability. When behaviors produce greater safety and predictability, it feels good to belong to that group or that department or the organization. Work life is more enjoyable even when work is challenging. When this is experienced on an emotional level, people will protect it. They will champion it because they care.

All of this is measurable. And when you catalyze the conversation around these principles that are demonstrated by behaviors that people see and experience, they will maintain the ground rules that they co-created to keep cooperation strong.

When employees are catalyzed to discuss the behaviors that build cooperation, the result is a common language and understanding. It is an empowerment process for front line employees that provides bottom up input for executive change planning and group process.

One leader expressed his appreciation for empowering his employees to define the behaviors that demonstrate trust, interdependence, genuineness, empathy, risk and success during the change process. He said the principles are simple and make common sense.

He equated it to a well built river raft that supported his employees as they paddled through treacherous rapids with dangerous whirlpools and submerged obstacles. It kept his employees in the boat and focused on what they were doing. It helped them take care of one another when they hit the rocks or needed to pick up the slack of someone who lost a paddle. Once in calm water they could regroup, express their appreciation for what the team did well, check their equipment, tighten their straps, pull the boat onto shore, climb to higher ground to scout the river ahead, then get back in the boat and charge ahead.

In this leader's view, the worst change experience happens when you have to change seats while you are in the rapids. Even if you don't know what you are doing, you can at least hold on tight and cheer the paddlers on.

The bottom line is that the behaviors your organization chooses to champion change can be taken into performance reviews. They can be used to assess leadership readiness. They can be used for performance based hiring processes. And they can be used for on-boarding new employees to maximize their work culture understanding and team fit. They can be used to analyze the effectiveness of your systems. Because these behaviors are readily visible in how people treat one another, how they cooperate on projects and how they treat the company and your customers, they are also measurable.

For this second take away, the behaviors that build cooperation during the change process support trust, interdependence, genuineness, empathy, risk and success. When your employees help to identify these behaviors they will be accountable to them. When you see employees demonstrating these behaviors in ways that streamline the change process, you can recognize them and tell new stories about it.

The Power Of Stories To Facilitate Change

This brings me to your third take away—why stories that surface during the change effort build momentum, sustain commitment and drive results remarkably fast.

In order for people to be engaged and accountable to champion change, there must be a vision of how the change will make things better than before. One reason two-thirds of all change efforts fail is that there is no follow up to keep the vision alive. Executives are great at coming up with goals, strategies and metrics. Unfortunately, they are sometimes notoriously bad at following up. Without follow up and recognition for small successes, employees will lose the vision of what achieving the change will feel and look like.

Another reason why two-thirds of change efforts fail is that few organizations actually reward the right behavior. Executive compensation plans, for example, often set the bar for making high salaries too low, which blurs the difference between success and failure. During the 2007 recession, for example, some executives received record level bonuses while their companies under performed.

Contemplating a change is much like standing on one side of a cliff, gazing over the abyss to the other side. The goal is to get to the other side with a new product, a new system, purchasing another company, changing your work culture to attract and retain top talent, making your company culture more cooperative or any number of other priorities.

In your communication action planning, stories highlight what is important and make the change vision come alive. Your senior employees have spent years learning how to succeed with a certain set of rules and they are playing to win. The rules were consciously put into place over the decades to support a system. When you proceed to change the system, you also change the rules mid-game.

Referring back to *Who Moved My Cheese?* and the two little people Hem and Haw, Haw is the little person who will change because he sees that change will be for the better. Hem won't budge because he is still invested in the old way. What is the fastest way to change a Hem into a Haw? The answer is simple: Peer pressure.

When I was researching what makes a group of people ethical, quality focused, productive, cooperative and successful, I discovered a study by a University of Illinois psychology researcher, Leann Birch. Leann conducted a series of experiments on children to see if she could get them to eat things they didn't like—specifically vegetables. This particular study focused on peas.

Bribing children who did not like peas with dessert didn't work. Explaining why peas were good for them didn't work. Demonstrating to a child how to eat peas didn't work. What did work repeatedly, however, was putting a child who hated peas at the table with children who loved peas. Within a meal or two, the child who hated peas started eating peas with the other children.

The rule of thumb is that people will conform to the behavior of the people around them because they want to belong. When this behavior involves winning with the new mid-game rules, other people will also try to win. When you follow through and recognize teams for small successes during the change process and share the stories of how they did it, others will soon figure out how to replicate it. They know what winning looks like. It becomes the better way of doing things.

Stories are also powerful when you recognize people for overcoming mistakes during the change process. You share how the mistake was made, how they resolved it at the root cause and what they learned in the process. When you share the story, other people hear it, learn from it and don't make the same mistake.

For example, if you want more civility, recognize people who went beyond the call of duty to be kind and helpful to someone in another department. If you want quality, recognize the rock star teams that achieve it and then tell stories about it to every new hire.

However, when you are standing on one side of the abyss, looking over to the other side and have not yet started your change effort, telling stories will seem unrealistic because everyone is still standing on the old side and performing the old ways. You have two choices when it comes to story telling. You can create a small step success that is dramatic and story-worthy based on the change you want to see. Then have other people tell the stories in the company about it at staff meetings and company gatherings. Or you can find stories in other organizations that represent the change you want to see and tell stories about them. You can invite leaders from that organization into your staff meetings to tell their stories.

Your third takeaway is that stories are very powerful. Employees will listen, strive to win and take action because of peer pressure. When employees champion change, tell stories often. Make it a part of new employee on-boarding. Make stories a part of your culture.

Capturing the emotional commitment of executives and employees is the key to engaging everyone to champion change. The three takeaways I have shared are emotionally intelligent social process tools that will engage employees to champion change remarkably fast.

TONY LACERTOSA, M.A.

About the Author

Tony Lacertosa, M.A. began his professional career as an educator and served as a mentor coach for colleagues who were struggling with classroom behavior and discipline problems.

Recognizing his ability to bring harmony to difficult group situations, Tony was asked to join a team of elite New York educators working with disengaged students in an alternative high school setting. Through effective behavior management strategies, students learned how to treat each other and themselves with respect resulting in a positive and successful school experience.

When he left teaching, Tony further developed his behavior management strategies for use in the workplace. Today, as founder of Peerless Leadership Development Consulting, he is committed to helping organizations improve their productivity through developing better relationships.

More information about Peerless Leadership Development Consulting is available on page 154.

Build Civility and Respect into Your Organization

To Improve Its Bottom Line

By Tony Lacertosa

If you discovered that the leaders of your organization spent about 13% of their time, which is over 6 weeks a year, resolving conflicts between employees, would you think there might be a problem that should be addressed? Do you think that those leaders could make better use of that month and a half of time?

A few years ago, Fortune magazine published the results of a survey of 1,000 executives who estimated that they spend about 6½ weeks a year resolving conflicts between employees. The situation has not improved much recently and might be even worse. In their well- researched 2009 book, *The Cost of Bad Behavior-How Incivility is Damaging Your Business and What to Do About It*, Christine Pearson and Christine Porath reported that 96% of people in the US have experienced incivility at work, more than half of them experienced stress as a result of it and three quarters of them are very dissatisfied by the way their company dealt with incivility.

Disconcerting as those numbers are, even more alarming is that while less than 1 person in 10 reported such incidents to the HR or Employee

Assistance Program departments of their companies, 9 out of 10 people who experienced incivility at work found a way to get back at their companies! Even with so many people retaliating against their employers, surveys show that many leaders are unaware and don't monitor the level of civility in their workplaces. Incivility and the stress it produces cost US companies as much as $300 billion dollars a year. It is time for businesses to pay closer attention to establishing a culture of civility if for no other reason than to improve their bottom line.

I congratulate you for recognizing the importance of this issue and for your interest in knowing more about it. Here are the four things you are about to learn: First, what is considered uncivilized behavior; second, how incivility may be affecting your organization's bottom line; third, how to build a culture of civil behavior in the workplace; and fourth, how to best handle incidents of incivility when they do occur. Without any further ado, let's get started.

Years ago, before becoming a consultant, I was a teacher in New York dealing with the high school students that most other teachers wanted out of their classrooms. These students were removed from the traditional school setting because they could not function properly in it. They would try to undermine the teacher's authority or find ways to disrupt the education of the other students. They had little respect for anyone else in the school and used what would be considered acts of incivility to get out of doing work or to get back at the school authorities for some perceived wrongdoing.

My first efforts in this alternative school setting were less than successful. I was coming home from work with all the stress-related ailments that go along with being in a situation where it felt as if everyone was out to make my life miserable. My reputation as a teacher was being compromised. My supervisors criticized me for having little control of the class and for my students' terrible academic results.

Knowing that I needed to make some big changes in how I managed my classroom, I decided go against the traditional advice of the day, which was to come off as being a tough guy and show no mercy until after Christmas vacation. It took changing my leadership style from tough guy to one based on strategies that foster mutual respect to save my career and earn me the reputation of a teacher who gets cooperation and improves productivity from formerly disruptive students. When I left teaching, I developed these strategies to apply to the workplace in order to help organizations improve their bottom line by establishing a cooperative, respectful and civil environment. These are the strategies that I am about to teach to you.

Let's start with the first thing I promised you would learn—what is considered uncivilized behavior. Most of us think of it in terms of someone being a bully or rude or perhaps displaying poor social skills. However, in terms of workplace incivility, we use a much broader definition. Some of the behaviors that employees consider to be uncivilized may surprise you, yet they are the actions that result in 50% of workers feeling they are treated uncivilly at work at least once a week.

What are these seemingly inconsequential actions that cause more than 90% of workers to do something to get even with their coworkers and their companies? Consider the examples given in *The Cost of Bad Behavior-How Incivility is Damaging Your Business and What to Do About It* by Pearson and Porath. The list they developed includes things such as the following:

- Taking credit for other people's work or blaming others for your mistakes
- Giving bad news by email rather than in person
- Not actively listening
- Spreading rumors or making derogatory remarks about others
- Setting up others for failure
- Not saying please, thank you or excuse me
- Showing up late for a meeting or leaving early

- Belittling or mocking others in words or body language
- Leaving snippy messages on voice mail
- Failing to return a phone call or email
- Shutting someone out of a network or team
- Throwing temper tantrums or yelling at people

As you can see from this list, the sense of being treated uncivilly is mostly a matter of how words or actions are perceived and how they make a person feel. You or anyone else in your organization may be guilty of committing some of these actions without even realizing that you did so or without any intent to be hurtful. However, those actions may have resulted in someone else feeling hurt and feeling that he or she was treated uncivilly.

At this point you may be thinking, "Oh come on, I am not going to watch every single thing I say and do to avoid potentially hurting the feelings of some employee. They're not babies, they need to develop a thicker skin and deal with life. They need to learn to suck it up."

If this is what you're thinking, I strongly caution you to consider the potential consequences of such an attitude. Companies where employees feel they are being treated uncivilly suffer in numerous ways that hurt them financially. Let's take a look at the second item I promised to teach you—how incivility and lack of respect in the workplace will hurt a company's bottom line and the reputation of its leaders.

It's important to realize that there are no inconsequential acts of incivility. Every action that is perceived by someone to be uncivilized will trigger negative responses often accompanied by some form of retaliation. Also, workers who merely *witness* acts of incivility will have the same negative reactions as the targets themselves such that an uncivil act toward one person may trigger retaliatory actions by several employees.

Workers experiencing or witnessing incivility on the job also report being less productive. They intentionally cut back on their work. In many cases they put in just the minimal amount of effort required to get the job done. Their motivation decreases while their level of anger increases. They spend time at work dwelling on the incident and how they will respond or get even with the offender.

These workers feel less valued and are less creative, often holding back their best ideas, and are less willing to help others. Teamwork suffers from a loss of trust between colleagues, from withholding information that is needed by the team, from a lost sense of interconnectedness and from a lowered commitment to the goals of the company.

Physically, workers who have experienced incivility on the job see an increase in stress-related illnesses. Exposure even to low levels of stress over time compromises the immune system, resulting in poor health among the company's workers, an increase in the number of sick days taken and higher health insurance costs. If any of these employees develops a long-term illness, you must also factor in the cost of hiring a replacement worker. And let's not forget about the increase in "mental health days" that we see when workers feel overly stressed and want a day or two to off to relax.

Sadly, most acts of incivility come from superiors, usually as some form of power play. This is especially troublesome for an organization because a subordinate might be afraid to report the incident for fear of suffering harm to his or her career. Instead, targets take out their frustration on someone further down the pecking order. Since leaders set the tone of an organization's culture, when employees are treated with incivility, they take out their frustrations by treating their coworkers uncivilly. Eventually this unacceptable behavior works its way into the customer service level. When customers are not treated nicely, word spreads quickly.

Customers who are treated uncivilly develop a poor image of the company. They not only feel uncomfortable themselves but also tell others of their bad experience, taking their business elsewhere.

The opposite is true as well. Look at companies who have a positive corporate image and about whom people have a good feeling and you see an organization where not only customers are treated with respect and civility, but where customers see the company's workers treating each other with the same respect. Southwest Airlines and Starbucks are two examples of such companies where civility and respect start from the top and trickle down through the entire organization with stellar results.

Still another way companies who are not committed to establishing a culture of respect and civility will suffer is in high employee turnover rates. A 2007 Gallup poll of more than a million workers found that the most common reason people gave for leaving their jobs was a stressful or problematic relationship with an immediate supervisor.

Retaining executives can be an issue as well. Studies have shown that the number one reason for the failure of executives is their own abrasive or bullying leadership style. The second reason for the failure of executives is an attitude of aloofness and arrogance. Executives who exhibit these traits often have problems because workers have little respect for these types of leaders and look for ways to see them fail. With the high cost of replacing employees and executives, retaining them by creating a culture of mutual respect and civility in the organization is vital to improving the bottom line.

There is also the very real possibility of lawsuits if uncivilized behavior is allowed to exist in a workplace. This kind of litigation is both costly and messy, providing another good reason to establish a culture of civility.

To be clear, civility is not about being nice or soft, it's about working with mutual respect. It is becoming ever more apparent that establishing such a culture in your company is vital to its current and future success. In his 2008 book *Choosing Civility*, Pier Massimo Forni, the award winning professor at Johns Hopkins University, founder and director of its Civility Initiative and collaborator in the Baltimore Workplace Civility Study, provides us with some food for thought. To quote from Professor Forni's book:

> No workplace in the world is as diverse as the American one. Fostering a workplace culture of civil openness and inclusion is clearly in the interest of most American organizations today. This is the

culture of the future, which will allow organizations to do well in the global civilization of the new millennium. It's not unreasonable to predict that lower-stress workplaces—workplaces, that is, where a culture of civility makes for better relationships among coworkers—will become very appealing. These are the workplaces where organizations will manage to attract and retain an increasing number of first-rate workers. This should be a strong incentive for organizations to promote a culture of civility in their workplaces.

Now that you have learned what constitutes uncivilized behavior and the various ways it can adversely affect your organization's bottom line, let's take a look at the third thing I promised to teach you—how to develop a culture of civility and respect in your organization. The key to developing such a culture comes down to implementing three strategies: Establishing policies, training employees and having leaders set good examples. Let's take a closer look at each one of these.

We'll start with establishing policies because all civility in the workplace begins with an organization setting and enforcing policies that show its commitment to civil behavior. Besides formally establishing the company culture regarding how it expects its employees to behave toward each other, clear company policies are needed to defend it should anyone file a law suit around any incivility issue. Courts have shown little mercy toward companies that do not have definitive written policies regarding how they expect their employees to behave.

There are a number of specific things that need to be in these policies. They must include the company's stance on anti-discrimination and anti-harassment along with any other expectations regarding the behavior of employees. They should also have a declaration of company values. Other things to put in a formal policy include a statement that the company has zero tolerance of uncivilized behavior, a complaint procedure and a statement that employees are expected to promptly file a complaint should an incident occur. This is all in addition to the other items usually found in company policies, such as how promotions, discipline and performance reviews are handled. Be sure that all formal policies comply with all federal, state and local laws.

One assumption organizational managers make is that giving their employees a policy booklet means they will actually read it, understand and remember all the policies. This is an unfortunate assumption because that rarely happens and often leads to misunderstandings that can turn into hard feelings and ugly situations. It is imperative that policies be reviewed with employees on a regular basis, at least once a year.

When it comes to establishing policies, leaders have a wonderful opportunity to show employees respect. One way is to be mindful of employees' feelings when making policies. Employees must understand that leaders are not being unreasonable in what they are asking of them, that leaders respect employees' personal time and space and they understand that employees are valuable human beings. When writing policies, leaders need to put themselves in the shoes of those who have to live by those policies. If the leader would not want to work under the conditions of a particular policy, neither will any of the other employees.

Another way leaders show employees respect when writing policies is to give them a voice in their formation. If an organization has established an environment of cooperation and mutual respect, employees will take this seriously and make valuable suggestions. When giving employees a voice in the policies, they see that their leaders value them, are considerate of their preferences and that they respect them. When employees have a say in the policies, they are more likely to take ownership of them.

The second strategy that I mentioned for building a culture of civility is employee training. Employees need to be taught what is expected of them and how to do their job. One of the major complaints employees have about their leaders is, "I was never taught what I needed to do yet I was blamed when it was not done properly." An employee who feels this way will definitely perceive that he or she was treated unfairly and harbor resentment as a result. About 25% of employees feel that they have not been properly trained for their jobs.

Also, don't assume employees know what constitutes civil behavior in the workplace. It is amazing how many of them simply don't know. Leaders must make clear to employees what behaviors are acceptable, which are not and the consequences of inappropriate behaviors. This should all be in the organization's policy statement.

Leaders need to be trained as well in things like how to spot signs of incivility and what to do about it. They also need to be taught communication skills, how to treat their employees with respect and how to coach them through rough patches. This brings us to the third strategy for building civility in organizations—seeing to it that leaders set good examples.

Leaders need to understand that the examples they set will filter all the way through the organization. I mentioned this earlier and am repeating it here for emphasis. If a leader's management style includes yelling and insulting, that behavior will trickle down and employees will yell and insult each other as well as customers. If you've ever been the victim of this behavior by customer service personnel as I have, then you know the bad taste it leaves in your mouth. Leaders with such abrasive personalities need to make style adjustments for the sake of their reputations, their own success and the benefit of the entire organization.

Leaders need to look in a mirror and ask for feedback on how their words and actions are being perceived. For example, they need to be sure that they speak in a respectful manner rather than yelling and barking out orders.

Other things leaders need to be aware of include the following:
- They need to say "Thank you" and "Please" and "Excuse me" and not just expect things be done for them because of their position of power in the organization.
- They must give credit where credit is due and show their appreciation for a job well done or for going above and beyond what is expected of an employee.

- They must be respectful of employees' personal space and personal time, being careful not to intrude on them whenever possible and to apologize when it is necessary.
- They must avoid combat and handle things calmly when dealing with conflict.
- They must show empathy when it is called for.
- They need to avoid micromanaging so as to give their employees the opportunity to be creative, to feel valued, to feel trusted and to take initiative.
- They must exhibit a real interest in their employees as people.

While it is important and necessary for leaders to recognize a job well done, they must also interact with their employees in ways that are not contingent on job performance. For example, a simple comment such as, "I see from the picture on your desk that your son plays little league baseball. How did he get interested in the sport?" adds a touch of humanity to the boss-worker relationship. "Is that a new car that I saw you drive into the parking lot this morning? Best wishes with it. What made you decide on that particular model?" is another example of a simple conversation that will go a long way in connecting with employees on a personal level that shows them they are valued as humans and not just as pawns in the organization. With the pressures of today's workplace it is easy to forget to connect with co-workers on a human level, but these non-work related conversations have to become a habit if leaders want to establish a culture of civility in their organizations.

At this point you may be thinking, "OK, even if our company does all the things you suggest, since such a small percentage of workers report incidents of incivility, how will we know if it is going on in our organization anyway and how do we handle it if it is?"

Let's take a look at this two-part question one part at a time. How do you know if incivility exists in your organization? You may not be absolutely certain, but a look at how things are going in the company can give you some good clues. Do you notice things such as unresponsive employees, lots of arguments, low employee morale, negative attitudes, increased customer service complaints or growing cultural and communication barriers among employees and customers? These are some of the things that may indicate you have problems to address.

If you observe these and similar productivity-killing conditions in your organization, you need to investigate them promptly. Perhaps an anonymous survey of what is going on will do the trick. Maybe reminding employees of the company policy on promptly reporting incidents of incivility and the consequences to the offender will bring people forward. In case uncivilized behavior is coming from someone in a supervisory position, it would be important for employees to know that they have a safe place to report the incident and that their careers will not be adversely affected by doing so. Again, all this needs to be spelled out in the company policies.

I cannot emphasize enough the importance of determining if the warning signs of trouble are a result of incivility or something else. If you are able to link the problem to uncivilized behavior you must pounce on it immediately, but in a way that will not cause employees to lose respect for the organization or its leaders.

How do you do that? Again, think mutual respect. No matter how upset a leader may be with an employee, remember that he or she will be more cooperative and not have the urge to push back if the leader remains calm and avoids going ballistic, especially in front of others. Hard as it may be for you to accept in the heat of the moment, it is important to help the offending employee save face in front of his or her colleagues

When I train leaders in how to have this conversation, I suggest that they begin by calmly telling the offender that they need to meet privately. Not only should the meeting itself be in private, but so should the request to speak with the person.

It is imperative that throughout the meeting the leader maintains composure. The proper tone of voice, body language and the words used should all set the required calm tone. Leaders must avoid accusations like, "You are creating a problem." It is better to say, "It seems that a problem is developing and I would appreciate your help in resolving it."

When the stage has been set to get into the specifics of the issue, the leader should begin by asking the offender what he or she did that created the need for a meeting. Hopefully the person will identify it. If not, the leader may have to point it out. If the employee denies any wrongdoing, the leader may have to get into a conversation about what constitutes uncivil behavior, which should be in the formal policies.

Once the specific act has been identified, ask the offender what he or she hoped to achieve by acting that way. A simple, "What did you hope to accomplish by saying what you said?" may make the person more aware of his or her motivations.

When the offender accepts what was done and why it was done, the leader then asks, "What should you have done instead?" This gets the offender to think about appropriate behavior. The meeting can be concluded by the leader asking, "What changes in your behavior are you willing to make so this can be a great place for everyone to work?" Be sure that all conversations are well documented to protect yourself and the company.

Are there going to be people who won't cooperate? Of course there will. Accept that these strategies will work in most situations and for most people. However, if you have an employee who just won't cooperate, you may have to consider termination. The saying that one bad apple can spoil the whole barrel definitely applies to these situations. Remember that if uncivilized behavior is allowed to continue, it will adversely affect an organization in the ways we already discussed. Everyone in the organization needs to understand that leadership will not tolerate uncivilized behavior and will promptly fire anyone who continues to engage in it.

To summarize, at this point you should have a better understanding of what behaviors are considered uncivilized, how incivility can hurt an organization and the individuals in it, how to build a culture of civility in your workplace and how to identify as well as deal with incivility when it occurs. If you still have doubts that your organization and its leaders can be hurt by allowing incivility to take place, just use Google to search "I hate my boss" or "I hate my job" to see what workers are saying publicly about their companies and supervisors. It may be quite an eye opening experience for you. Be sure that your organization and its leaders don't show up in any of those Google searches. Establishing a culture of civility and mutual respect will go a long way in making sure that doesn't happen.

MICHAEL BOUTON

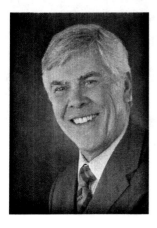

About the Author

Michael Bouton has over 15 years in assessment consulting for selecting the most appropriate talent and team development programs. Prior to that Michael founded two companies successfully through acquisition and played primary in the positioning and growth of start up operations.

For the past 10 years Michael has developed team building workshops and selection services that are delivered worldwide through a network of trained facilitators and coaches.

The majority of Michael's clients are fortune 500 multinational companies.

During his long career Michael has written many articles the most recent on using psychometric tools to help make the right hire published in The Journal of Medical Practice Management November/December 2011 issue.

More information about Michael and his company is available on page 156.

Tuckman's 5 Stage Team Development Model

From 4 Months to 1 Day

By Michael Bouton

There is a common problem in many organizations today that is leading to poor team performance. I know my son experienced it personally several years ago when he took over a new management position in an IT department for a state government. In his first review as a manger he was lauded for his very capable technical skills, but criticized for his lack of managerial capability. At the time I asked him how much training he had in management skills. "None" was his answer. How often are people put into a position to fail due to a lack of training, especially in fields where the people drawn to them may not be blessed with the best people skills? What can be done to assist organizations to provide better management and leadership training so that their people become more proficient and understand the team dynamics that will increase performance?

The Need for High-Performing Teams

A large field of research has proven that teams are crucial to the success of all organizations, from small local businesses to large global conglomerates. The challenges, however, are finding ways to better lead and manage teams to reach higher performance.

Many years ago Bruce Tuckman proposed his four-stage model of group development (now 5 stages). He noted that all groups go through the phases and, while they may go back and forth between the stages, he noted how important each stage was for the team to grow and develop properly. He also noted that when things did not go smoothly in any one of the stages, the team could get stuck and performance would drop.

It can take a great deal of time to develop high-performing teams and there is a need for leaders to govern those teams to address cohesion and conflict management. The information that follows will cover each of the 5 stages of the Tuckman model and how managers can be taught to use behavior assessments and team training to advance through each stage more thoroughly and more efficiently.

1. **Forming:** Increase personal understanding and reduce negative judgments.
2. **Storming:** Reduce negative relationship conflicts to increase cohesion.
3. **Norming:** Comprehend the need for norms that will increase productivity.
4. **Performing:** Utilize the strengths of each behavioral style to make sure needed roles are filled.
5. **Adjourning:** Identify areas for improvement for future work.

Why do teams fail?

Here are three areas courtesy of Dale Perryman that affect team performance, even to the point of failure.

1. Leadership—Lack of agreement around what is important
2. A lack of clarity around roles and responsibilities
3. Conflict among the team—primarily behavioral

Looking first at leadership, results from a survey revealed that the issues revolve around vision and mission, lack of clear understanding of what the organization is trying to achieve and why, lack of enthusiasm about goals and no clear line of sight between tasks and goals. Those translate into trust, communication and work satisfaction problems. Having good to great team leaders is absolutely critical towards engagement, retention and growth. As we'll see exploring Tuckman's Five Stages, leadership plays a critical part in the first and second stages. After that, if the die has been properly cast, the team needs less attention from the leader as they are attuned to what needs to be done and by whom in order to achieve their goals, resulting in a high level of performance.

Forming

In the forming stage of team building, it is all about being accepted by the others and avoiding controversy or conflict. Serious issues and feelings are avoided and people focus on being busy with routines such as team organization, assigning roles and duties, when to meet and so on. But individuals are also gathering information and forming impressions about each other, about the scope of the task, and about how to approach it. This is a comfortable stage to be in, but the avoidance of conflict and threat means that not much actually gets done. The leader plays a part in directing the team and setting out some ground rules such as the following:

1. We will encourage open and honest discussion.
2. We will show respect for one another and not engage in personal attacks.
3. We will actively participate.
4. We will listen attentively to what others have to say.

Even though the stage has been set, a group left on its own to integrate themselves into a new team environment can cause some initial difficulties because of unknowns. Assuming that this team is brand new, with few if any established relationships, getting to know each other can be fun, but it can also set up some personality clashes. From the brain's perspective, each individual is attempting to determine if the other team members will be potential friends or foes.

One way the brain can navigate these relationships is by learning the language of behavior, which is a readable, logical, and understandable language. All of us have a distinct amalgamation of four behavioral characteristics: Dominance (D) or how you handle problems, Influence (I) or how you handle people, Steadiness (S) or how you handle pace, and Conscientiousness (C) or how you handle procedures/constraints. By using the language of behavior people are better able to understand behavioral clues that they react to adversely. Understanding those clues and why they affect you negatively can assist in the reprogramming of the brain to accept team members as friends. The closer your behavioral style is to another's, the easier it is for you to get along socially. Interestingly, that same relationship may not be as harmonious or productive in a work team environment. Understanding the language of behavior enables people to separate the message from the way it's delivered, moderating the emotional experience and preventing potentially adverse reactions.

The forming stage is the best place to incorporate an assessment-based behavioral workshop. The language of behavior is an easy language to learn. An assessment that accurately describes your behavioral style including your strengths, ideal work environment, communication patterns and more will reinforce what you already know. Taking the next step in understanding how your behavioral style affects people with different behavioral styles is where the opportunity for leaping to the next level of team performance begins. By sharing this information with other team members and vice versa, all of the team members have the option to modify their behavioral style to better fit the expectations of people with a different style for enhanced communication and understanding. This sharing also results in a better understanding of how the differing styles enhance the potential of the whole team.

We are not suggesting that conflict be avoided. We are saying that conflict can be far less uncomfortable and more productive by removing behavioral misunderstandings. The team leader gains insight into each member's strengths so that tasks and responsibilities can be more effectively assigned. The assessment can done for a relatively small cost, about four hours of time invested and may even be facilitated by one of your own employees. This return on investment overshadows the cost significantly in productivity and engagement. It always amazes me the relative ease with which we can justify the purchase of equipment that promises productivity increases, but we often have a very hard time employing simple yet extremely effective methods to improve the productivity of people through soft-skills training.

In the forming stage the team leader plays a critical role. One objective is to frame the outcome the team is to accomplish—call it the team's vision/mission. Another objective is on task directing, focusing the team on what needs to be done to accomplish goals. The team needs high direction at this point, but how that is delivered can be supportive or destructive.

Years ago I attended a practical leadership workshop based on music. Our goal as a team was to create a musical score for a video. The first time I participated in this workshop, an experienced team leader or producer led it. He directed us through the process of developing a clear understanding of what we were trying to achieve and the path we would be taking to achieve it. This producer-facilitated process with all the team's involvement yielded a result that was very clear about our end goal. We had a clear vision and mission. Involving us in the creation of that vision gave us ownership in what we were about to embark upon. The second time I participated in the same workshop there was no producer. The members of this workshop were comprised mostly of an existing team with existing leadership. With the exact same problem to solve as in the first workshop, this leadership team decided that they were the ones to create the vision and mission and then dictate to us—the worker bees. That did not feel good, nor were we very engaged. Their constant meddling, lack of trust and micromanagement disengaged many team members to an extreme level. Unlike the first experience in this workshop, we felt devalued. In the first workshop what we accomplished was incredible. The second workshop produced a miserable outcome.

Storming

Here is where significant relationship (i.e., interpersonal) conflict can surface. Different ideas compete for consideration. The team addresses what problems to solve, how they will function independently and together and task assignment among others. Confrontation regarding ideas and perspectives erupt. In some cases, storming can be resolved quickly. In others, the team never leaves this necessary stage. It can be contentious, unpleasant and even painful to conflict-averse members of the team. This is where the emotional maturity of team members determines whether the group will ever move out of this stage. If a team continues to storm, it will not develop norms that support teamwork. This low level of teamwork will probably result in the team not achieving its stated goal. Once again, understanding behavioral language and using it can greatly facilitate this process.

The team leader during this phase is still in a directive mode, but needs to show support and perhaps even provide coaching so that team members can resolve their differences comfortably with one another. Part of the problem in this phase is the battle over status. Threats to status will reduce cohesion. A good leader who understands behavioral styles will recognize each style's status threats and make sure respect is maintained. One idea is to promote the feeling that they are not being judged so they will be more comfortable sharing their opinions and views. Keep in mind that a negative judgment is a threat to status. The language of behavior coupled with emotional intelligence can mean the difference between success and mediocrity. This phase can be destructive to the team and lower motivation if allowed to get out of control.

During the storming phase most conflicts will center on task and personalities. During this phase the leader should establish parameters to develop high-performing teams such as the following:

1. Acknowledge the importance of task work and teamwork from the outset.
2. Create ground rules for group behavior in the first meeting and follow them.
3. Develop a shared vision of the group goal.
4. Use collaborative processes throughout this stage.
5. Use the action/research cycle to guide data collection and decision-making.
6. Manage conflict when it arises.
7. Involve users in the process from the outset.

Once again the ideal management style for the leader is a combination of a "high concern for task" and a "high concern for people." High-performing teams have low to moderate levels of task conflict assuming high levels of agreement on the goal or vision at the outset and healthy discourse regarding various alternatives for achieving the goal, resulting in agreement on the team's output. I might also add that understanding behavioral task preference can assist the leader in assigning tasks. On the relationship side, teams on the path to high performance will have low levels of relationship conflict, although there will always be some as project deadlines approach.

In relationship conflict you have the extroverts overwhelming the introverts, the directs compromising the in-directs, fast-paced pushing the slower and the task-focused impatient with the people-focused. All of

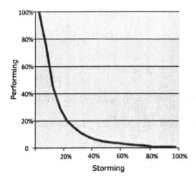

these combinations of behavioral styles are operating in the pressurized environment of the team to get its act together, causing conflict just because people are different and act differently. But wait, isn't that what we addressed in the forming stage?

Using the DISC model we have four primary behavioral styles. The way a person deals with problems is referred to as dominance (D). A person that is very high dominant will attack problems aggressively, driving for results with a high degree of impatience. They address problems confrontationally. For lots of people influence, the interpersonal (I) style is predominant. People that are high in this style are interactive, enthusiastic, verbally proficient, somewhat exaggerative, have low attention to detail, want to get things done through people and are creative. High dominant and high influential people are very fast-paced and direct. The steadiness (S) style deals with pace. High steadiness people have a tendency to be resistant to change. They are very methodical, preferring to finish one task before proceeding to the next. This ability to adhere to a process makes them very effective in getting things done. Good listeners and patient, they are the glue that holds the team together. The conscientious (C) style has a preponderance to adhere to established rules and procedures as well as attention to details. The high conscientious individual will have a tendency to be very critical of ideas as well as themselves. Both the high S and the high C are indirect and slower-paced.

Few people are strictly one style. We are all a combination. However, those of us very high in one or two styles can easily create difficulty in communication, expectations and appreciation. For example, the high D people are critical team members because of their drive to get results, but can be difficult because their way of addressing a problem is to confront it head-on. That direct confrontational style works well with another high

D, but all of the other styles do not react in a positive manner, setting up uncomfortable interactions. All of the styles have their preferred means of communication, positive ways to communicate with them and communication cues you should definitely stay away from. Knowing this can facilitate the transmission of information without the adverse effects of behavioral reaction.

Addressing the behavioral style language in the forming stage prevents these very tense and stressful conflicts. Keeping the language alive is another responsibility of the leader. Reinforcing what the team has learned about each other and using the language is a continuing exercise. The better the expertise the better the outcome. Remember that we are emotional beings and one negative emotional event brought on by insensitive behavior can take hours to recover from. Two negative emotional events and you are done for the day.

Let's integrate this idea with how the brain works. In the storming stage, contentious outbreaks between team members can cause the brain to consider other team members as foes. As David Rock points out in his book, *Your Brain at Work*, "When you think someone is a foe, you don't just miss out on feeling his emotions; you also inhibit yourself from considering his ideas, even if they are right. When you decide someone is a foe, you tend to discard his ideas, sometimes to your detriment." The trick here is to minimize an adversarial environment so that team members are not seen as foes but as friends.

Norming

This stage puts it all together and the team slips into a routine that maximizes their individual talents. Here is where the leader can reinforce actions by complementing or giving recognition to individual members. The leader is also on the lookout for individuals that are showing initiative and extra effort that might be rewarded with projects on their own or a leadership position. The leader also needs to be noticing those that are slacking off and unengaged to spend some effort understanding what may be causing it and possibly coaching to remedy the situation. A last resort might be to remove those actively disengaged underperformers to prevent them from having an adverse effect on the other members of the team.

Returning to the leadership workshop illustration in the storming stage above, our producer skillfully led us through that stage and gave us a positive feeling towards our objectives. Now let's take a look at the second workshop. As we moved through the activity the management team took to dictating what they saw and what should be done rather than involving us. As a result individual team members felt devalued, de-motivated, uninterested and basically checked out. Remember the objective of this workshop was to put a musical score to a video. It just so happened that one of the team members had experience as a musician and the management team focused all their attention on that one individual so that their created content would be higher, thus maximizing the incentive bonus. The downside was that all this attention on one person left the rest of the team out of the picture. This team never got to the norming or performing stages because all the emphasis was based on one star and the outcome was a disaster.

Performing

In this stage high-performing teams are able to function as a unit as they find ways to get the job done smoothly and effectively without inappropriate conflict or the need for external supervision. By this time they are motivated and knowledgeable. The team members are now competent, autonomous and able to handle the decision-making process without supervision. Dissent is expected and allowed as long as it is channeled through means acceptable to the team.

The team leader during this phase is just maintaining and should not push too hard, which can cause potential burn out and resentment. An injection of fun is important and using the DISC language the leader seeks out those individuals whose strongest style is influential for their ideas regarding fun activities.

Having successfully led the team through the preceding three stages, the team leader can effectively delegate most of the necessary decisions, only acting when asked. Keep in mind that even the highest-performing teams can revert to earlier stages in certain circumstances. Most long-standing teams go through these cycles many times as they react to evolving circumstances. For example, a change in leadership may cause the team to revert to storming as the new people challenge the existing norms and dynamics of the team. New members replacing exiting members can also cause the team to revert. Once again the leader is key to holding it together and guiding the team back to the performing stage.

Let's go back to the leadership workshop one last time. As we went through the second and third stages of producing our part of the music, team members became very comfortable with their roles and the objective. During each of these stages we all played different roles, one of which was manager of the team. During the third session I had the role of manager. Using my experience as a manager, I felt the necessity of inserting myself in the process. I needed to be part of the experience, adding my expertise and knowledge to make the process go smoother. Unfortunately, for me anyway, when I tried to do this the team collectively said, "we understand our roles, we clearly see the objective, and right now we don't need you." Imagine how I felt. I was rejected! I slunk back to a corner, sat down and reflected on my team's rejection. It was then I realized this was a gift. We were in the performing stage. I did not have to expend energy trying to herd team members towards the objective because that had already been accomplished earlier. This left me free to focus on other areas of importance.

Adjourning and Transforming

In 1977, Tuckman and Jensen worked together to add a fifth stage to the original four stages. This covers the end of a project and the breakup of the team. This can also be the time when a member leaves and a new member joins, bringing the team back to a very short episode in the forming stage. This stage was the reason behind the music video workshop used in my examples. Some folks at a very large electronics company, who coincidentally played together in a band, noticed the extreme dissatisfaction when teams got to this stage. A common remark was, "We did a great job in achieving our goal but I never want to do that again with this team." As a result of studying that outcome, they developed their "Practical Leadership" music-based workshop. The idea was to show how inspirational leadership shaped the experience into a positive result. We had fun and produced a great outcome in the first workshop, but not so much in the second.

Observations

How teams traverse the stages will determine their ultimate success as a team. Without good leadership encompassing emotional competency, experience and good judgment, a team can take an inordinate amount of time getting through the stages and might not ever get to a high-performing level.

In the practical leadership music-based workshop we barely got out of the first stage in the second example and the end result was a disaster. Although workshops are not the real world, they do illustrate some important points. First is the importance of clearly understanding what the team is about, its vision. Second is that establishing the rules and guidelines of the team and the function of the leader greatly reduces the task conflict that could otherwise erupt in the absence of such structure.

In the storming stage conflict is a very necessary part of arriving at the best ideas. How that conflict is managed will chart the way towards performance or keep the team mired in mediocrity. Avoiding conflict results in less successful outcomes and ignoring conflict quite often leads to a dead end, but applying established tools such as the language of behavior to encourage understanding and effective communication can greatly reduce the interpersonal strife often experienced in the storming stage. Don't forget the importance of having fun. It has been shown that putting some fun into the workplace unleashes more creativity.

Finally

A couple of closing notes: The designers of the Practical Leadership music-based workshop wanted to incorporate DISC because they recognize its value. Having been champions of the language of DISC in both leadership programs and team development in their company, they see the benefits of including it in any team development program. In this chapter we have focused on leadership and the language of DISC as ways to shorten and smooth the journey through Tuckman's five stages. As advances in technology level the playing field, the last frontier for getting a competitive edge lies in how you lead and manage people. As Robert S. Hartman once said, "Treating your employees first as people then as employees can unleash up to 40% more productivity." Selecting leaders that have this embedded into their personality and making it part of your culture can pay amazing dividends. You only have to look at a company like Zappos to see the results. There are other complementary tools to DISC that can help you realize this goal. With that in mind do not miss the chapter *Human Performance From the Inside Out* by Pam Brooks for a look at putting together the strongest and most appropriate team possible.

PAMELA BROOKS, M.A.

About the Author

Pamela Brooks, M,A, is a human performance specialist that has been working with individuals, teams, and companies on ways to improve their relationships, leadership, and performance for the past 10 years. Her passion for understanding human performance started as a collegiate athlete and has continued to grow through her time as a collegiate advisor, coach and instructor.

Pam has conducted numerous trainings on understanding performance potential and relationships for HR.com, in her work with the University of Phoenix and as an instructor at Arizona State University. She has also been helping companies with their onboarding of new employees to find ways to bring the employees up to speed quicker and improve their performance potential within the organization.

Pam is the founder of Cornerstone Consulting.

More information about Cornerstone Consulting is available on page 158.

Human Performance from the Inside Out

by Pam Brooks

My passion for understanding human performance started during my collegiate athletic career and has never stopped. I felt the pain when athletes dropped off their teams and out of school. They were recruited for their passion to play and their talent but left feeling like failures. Is this to be expected in a competitive environment where only the strong survive? Is it just another risk you're expected to take like in organizations today?

The NCAA saw turnover and low graduation rates as a bad thing and took measures to successfully reduce the negative impact. Unfortunately, no governing body exists that can insist that turnover be reduced in organizations; the EEOC can only enforce that it is *equally* felt by all. While many successful organizations realize that turnover is felt in the cost of replacement, from a conservative $13,500 estimate by the Bureau of Labor and Statistics (O'Connell & Mei-Chuan, 2007) to $7,000 + a day by many placement organizations. High turnover, especially at the executive level, also leads to poor company morale, image and stock prices. In small organizations, turnover can even cause a company to fold.

Not all turnovers are bad, and not all of the reasons for turnover can be eliminated, but there is much that can still be done to improve the selection and onboarding process of employees to ensure higher retention and performance rates. One of the controllable issues related to early job turnover in companies is the shock factors that lead people to terminate. These "shocks" are created by the gaps between expectations and the reality of what exists on the job (Holtom, Mitchell, Lee, & and Inderrieden, 2005). Many these shocks result from human bias in the selection process by both the employer and the employee. They can range from the neglect of properly defining job roles, misrepresentations and anticipation of performance levels, poor job fit between a new hire and company culture, and/or a disconnect with a manager or work team. Understanding the keys to human performance can be life changing and by creating more objective job expectations, many of the potential shock factors can be greatly reduced while at the same time increasing satisfaction and engagement. The following areas will be covered in this chapter:

- Why bias exists in the selection process.
- How to remove bias from the selection process.
- Understanding the fundamental influences on human performance from the outside in.
- Measures for human performance from the inside out.

Why Bias Exists in the Selection Process

To better understand how bias enters the selection process, here is a hypothetical staffing situation in a medium-sized company. Sue is the HR Specialist and has been asked by the CEO to find a new manager for a department because the present manager will be leaving for personal reasons. Sue is told she has three weeks to fill the position, but she knows in reality that this means she needs the top candidates lined up in just two weeks. Like any HR person, she has many pressing projects to work on—from new health directives to employee training courses. She starts her regular routine for the job search by finding the job description for the position. She notes that it should be updated as it is a couple years old, but does not feel she has the time to deal with it and still uses it as the basis for posting the job opening in the local paper and with online job boards. After posting the position, the vice president stops in to chat about the management position and tells her a few of the ideas he has about some new responsibilities he would like the position to take over. She takes a mental note of this and then goes on with her tasks. By mid-week the word is out that there is a management opening and the COO comes by to tell Sue that he has the perfect candidate for the job, telling her some new things he would like the manager in that department to take over. Sue is always intimidated by the COO, so she writes down what he said and is very conscious of taking the name down of the COO's recommen-dation. By this time she has received over 30 applications for the position and has started a folder for them to review later. She has also had a couple of internal candidates stop by to ask about the job and she knows they are eager to get a promotion. She has nothing better to give them than the old job description.

STOP: How much bias exists already with a poor job description, two different executives wanting to make different changes to the position? Then there is the potential bias towards internal candidates and the intimidating COO pushing for his own candidate. But even more importantly, the time pressure that Sue feels to fill the job quickly has greatly reduced her objectivity.

By the end of week one Sue is stressing about the situation because she must narrow the field of candidates for the CEO, VP and COO before the end of week 2. She takes the work home with her over the weekend and sets up evaluative criteria based on the job description for education, recent experience, turnover and background, along with what the COO suggested from her notes. Sue still does not feel comfortable rating the 60+ potential candidates as she knows there will be many well-qualified people and always feels bad about turning some of them away. Half way through the stack she gets bored with reviewing and just wants to get to her own home projects. She happens to catch the resume of the COO's candidate and puts it on the top of the potential stack because the individual meets the minimum qualifications and obviously has an inside recommendation. By the time she finishes her review she is sick of reading resumes but has probably only given each one about a 6-second look for minimum qualifications before deciding to include or exclude it in final count (Giang, 2012).

By the middle of Week 2 Sue has narrowed the field of candidates down to 6. They all seem to have good recommendations, experience, and education. Two of them are from inside the company, so a lot is known about them, and one is the COO's pick who also has good experience and recommendations. A meeting is then set with the CEO, COO and VP to review the candidates before doing official background checks. The group likes Sue's criteria, but the VP and COO each manage to add a few extra criteria based on their ideas for the new manager. They each review the candidates quickly and pick their top three. The VP is excited to see one of the internal candidates in the pool as he knows he has been working hard. At the end of 30 minutes they narrowed the pool to 4. In the final pool are one internal candidate, the COO's recommendation and two others that will now be interviewed.

STOP: At this point the criteria have been changed and there is more personal bias towards two of the potential candidates. Meanwhile, the initial criteria were based on the old job description. There is danger at this point that a qualified candidate might have been left out, given the shifts in criteria.

After background checks, the next step will be interviews. While some information is gained during these, most interviews are full of personal bias unless the interviewer knows how to ask the right questions and has very clear criteria. Companies would be better off tossing a coin to predict productivity on the job than trying to determine it through a personal interview. Studies have shown that simply being extroverted has been related to interview success (Caldwell & Burger, 2006) even though it is not a predictor of true job performance. Add to this the biases in the scenario above of people knowing the potential candidates, the natural tendency for candidates so say the "right" things to present themselves in the best light, and the natural tendency of all humans to like the people who are most like themselves and you have a recipe for many potential mismatches or "shocks" when the person finally comes on board. While not all of these biases may happen in every hiring situation, many occur on a regular basis.

How to Remove Bias in the Selection Process

Every good business decision should have a set of defined criteria to evaluate options, much like buying a new chair or a piece of software for your office. The same should be true in staffing. The *Structure of Value* (Hartman, 1967) provides a disciplined framework to ensure that all of the key areas of the job are examined in the categories of *people, process* and *systems*. These core areas cover all aspects of a job and have been proven to be the cornerstones in top organizations described in *Good to Great* (Collins, 2001) and *Firms of Endearment* (Sisodia, Wolfe, & Sheth, 2007). Using job rubrics to break down performance in the three core areas creates a visual standard of how much talent is needed in which areas and how much time will be spent performing specific skill sets. Rubrics have been proven to add more objectivity in measuring performance (Reddy, 2011).

Job rubrics should be the first thing developed with the participation of all key people working around the open position. While many feel they don't have the time, when done correctly this process will be the most valuable time spent. Rubrics can actually speed up the initial screening process and will produce more objective results because there are clear standards by which to compare and contrast the candidates. The added bonus is that potential candidates will be given a more realistic picture of the job itself. *To find out how to get more information on the job rubrics and how to use them, see the Appendix.*

Let's revisit the hypothetical staffing situation and see how it plays out with the use of job rubrics. Sue realizes when she is asked by the CEO to find a new manager for a department that the long term outcome of this hire is more important than just the short term push to fill a position. In her training on using job rubrics she discovered that a little quality time up front will save her a great deal of time and confusion about the future expectations of the position.

Instead of looking for the job description, she immediately sends an email with the job rubrics and instructions to each of the key players that interact with the position, such as the CEO, COO and VP (Lehrer, 2012). She also sends them to the current manager because this individual will be able to give very clear insight into the current position. Sue gives everyone a deadline of two days to return the information to her and requests that they have a short meeting in the afternoon of the third day to review the compiled information. Her mind is much freer now to continue working on her other important projects.

At the end of the second day she is able to quickly compile the information she has gained from each of the individuals and completes master job rubrics for each area, making sure to note any potential contradictions or differences. In the meeting Sue covers what was gained from compiling the rubrics and targets discussion around the differences in opinion. These discussions prove to be important as the COO and VP realize that they had potentially conflicting ideas for the future of the position. With the help of the CEO they are able to reach a compromise and clear up the potential conflicts so that everyone has very clear expectations. The COO, who thought he had a potential candidate for the position, realizes that the person would not be a good fit given the clear criteria upon which they have agreed.

With the completed rubrics Sue is able to write a very clear job description that targets the key aspects of the job. She then posts this in the newspaper and the usual online job boards. Half way through week 2 Sue has received at least 30 applicants and has been easily screening them based on the solid rubrics that have been set up. She had several people within the company come by to ask about the open position during the week and she was able to give them the rubrics to determine their own potential fit. She noted in the end that only one internal person applied and did a great job of addressing the key aspects of the job in the cover letter. By the end of week two Sue is able to set up a meeting to give the CEO, COO and VP the top 5 candidates to review. After this meeting they agree on the top three and ask Sue to have their backgrounds checked and to have them assessed further, so that they can be sure to target their interviews with the individuals. *Note: For some companies, taking the time for rubrics may not be enough. You may also want to hire an outside placement consultant to fully measure many other key aspects of the organizational culture and leadership team to ensure the best fit. See Chapter 6: Hire for Fit versus Hire for Fill.*

Understanding the Fundamental Influences on Human Performance from the Outside In

Scientists have determined that the best way to predict a person's future performance potential is by looking at their past. Taking the time to explore the fundamentals of where a person came from gives you a better idea of where they may go in the future. The first influence to understand from the past is fundamental genetics or what a person is born with, commonly called *natural talent*. When people are given the opportunity to develop their natural talents they will excel and make it look effortless. Natural talent can lie in areas such as working with people, performing different tasks, problem solving, or being able to organize and set a vision for the future. The second area of influence comes from actual *experience*.

Not everyone has the potential to be a Beethoven, but had Beethoven not been given the opportunity to be around music, would we know about him today? As noted in the book *Outliers* by Malcolm Gladwell, it takes 10,000 hours to create an expert or specialist in any line of work, and the mere exposure at an early age in any given field or calling gives a person the potential for greater development (Gladwell, 2008). Take, for example, the story of Wilma Rudolph, a girl who could not walk at an early age because of deformities in her legs. She was so determined to overcome this that she eventually became one of the fastest women in track and field. To reach this level, however, she needed more than time spent running. She also needed expert guidance, which leads into the last area influence from the past, the *knowledge* we gain from larger societal and cultural norms. We learn our place in the world and gain knowledge from what we are told by parents and coaches, from the rules and norms we learn through observation, and others picked up from our formal education, training and places we have worked.

Given the importance of talent, experience and knowledge, it is critical to cut through what is said to identify what is *proven*. Instead of looking at the resume for a reason to exclude it, you should be looking at the resume for a reason to keep it. Does the candidate have *demonstrated* talent, experience or knowledge in the areas you need? The correct way to read a resume is in chronological order, so start from the back and read forward if the most current information is first. This will help you get a clearer idea of how the person has progressed. Some things to look for which demonstrate past success in each area include the following:

- **Talent:** Excels quickly, accomplishments in progressive order, excels with increased responsibility, enjoys increased challenges in the area of talent
- **Experience:** Look for measurable results, proven accomplishments, awards won in the talent area, length of time spent in years without gaps, direct responsibility that can be proven,

- **Knowledge:** Has correct level of education, has continued education and growth and shows applied knowledge of training in their work, or increased responsibility in their work post training

Another way to gain understanding about an individual's talent, experience and knowledge is through targeted interview questions. It is best not to use hypothetical situation questions because the interviewee will only tell you what you want to hear. It is better to ask direct questions that relate back to the personal experience listed on the resume. It is harder to fudge what you have actually done than it is to create what you would do. Remember that a proven past is the best predictor of the future. Here are some questions you might ask to get at proven ability in each of the areas:

- **Talent:** Tell me about your greatest talent and how you applied it in your last position? What would your last boss say was your greatest talent and why? What have you done to develop your greatest talent?

- **Experience:** What was the greatest project for which you were responsible? How did you go about planning it? What was the greatest challenge you had to overcome? What was the most difficult team you have had to work with? What are the 3 most significant accomplishments in your career so far? Who was the best manager you have worked for and why? Who was the worst manager and why? What is a typical day at work like for you? What type of criticism and/or advice have you been given and how did you deal with it?

- **Knowledge:** What was the greatest piece of information you learned from your formal education and/or training that you were able to apply in your most recent position? What additional trainings have you acquired on our own or through work? How did you incorporate your new knowledge in your position? What was your biggest mistake and what did you learn from it?

These types of questions, especially when targeted around the key areas identified in the job rubrics, will give you a much clearer idea of a person's ability based on past experience to perform particular skills on the job in the future. If they had a problem with a specific type of person, task, or rule that you have in your company, they may not be a good fit!

Objective Measures of Human Performance Potential From the Inside Out

Using some form of screening assessment can increase both objectivity in selection and the ability to find more qualified candidates (Jansen, 2005). Detailed assessments can give a better idea of a person's talents, skills and knowledge by evaluating them from the *inside out*. You get a real picture of what they are like from directly testing what is on the inside that influences their outside actions. The right assessments will allow you understand how the person will be on the job and what factors affect their performance. Good assessments should provide you with objective measures about the individual's strengths and limits as well as potential interview questions for how to get at potential weaknesses. In many instances you may need multiple assessments to objectively measure the core areas. While assessments may cost money, this cost is relatively small compared to the cost of a bad hire.

Remember that the assessments need to give insight into the areas related to the job rubrics, those being people, task and system/planning. Three different assessment categories are found below:

1. Motivational Assessments:
   a. Indicate why a person may want to perform a job or task.
   b. If the job will give them satisfaction in their highest motivational areas, it may be a good fit.
   c. If the job will not give satisfaction for the individual's core areas,

it could result in a shock over time that leads the candidate to find other work.

    d. Some examples of these assessments are the *Personal Interest, Attitudes and Values (PIAV) and Business Motivators*, both of which are great for also capturing executive team culture.

2. Behavioral Assessments:

    a. These are sometimes mislabeled as personality tests. In reality they measure an individual's way of interacting with the world and dealing with such things as problems, people, pace of life and procedures.

    b. They are the most common form of assessment on the market and often measure a person's tendency towards introversion or extroversion along with relationship or task orientation. They help you understand how a person will respond after a few months on the job. Most people will attempt to be more extroverted for an interview and more compliant in their first months.

    c. The reports are often good at providing strengths and limitations about the individual as well as interview questions.

    d. While they should never be used alone to predict a perfect job fit, they can provide valuable information on a person's natural behavioral fit to the job.

    e. Some examples of these tests are *DISC* (over 25 different brands on the market), *Enneagram, Myers Briggs* (MBTI), the *Big 5 Personality* and *Kolb* reports.

3. Judgment or Thinking Style Assessments:

    a. These assessments attempt to let you know how a person processes information.

    b. There are many different types in the market that range from intelligence type tests like the *Wounderlic* to emotional intelligence assessments like the *E-IQ*.

   c. There are also deductive instruments that measure an individual's judgment or thinking style based on the *Hartman Value Profile* (HVP) and the *Science of Valuation* mentioned earlier.

   d. These reports can directly measure ability in each of the three core areas of people, task and system and give measures for internal self-awareness, an individual's understanding and devotion to their job/role and their internal drive to see and go after personal goals.

   e. For more information on HVP report distributors, visit the Hartman Institute website at http://www.hartmaninstitute.org/AxiologicalServiceProviders.aspx.

Using a combination of these assessments that measure motivation, behavior and thinking will give you a more objective perspective of what a person will bring to the job from the inside out. When you combine this information in the areas of people, task and systems with what you can get from an individual's resume and interview related to their talent, experience and education, you can get a more objective view of how they relate to the essential elements on the job rubrics you have created. You can actually place each candidate on the rubrics to see where and how well each candidate lines up with the job. With the information you gain from the assessments you can also target your training for the hired individual to help reduce the potential for future "shocks" and to ensure that the individual reaches higher performance levels faster. You will be able to help candidates maximize their strengths and minimize potential limitation.

I have been using a combination of these reports for screening and coaching during the past 10 years and they have proven to be excellent predictors of how a person will perform on the job. They are excellent tools for improving onboarding practices and training. They are also helpful in identifying areas for improvement in executive team leadership, especially when addressing the results of a TIGERS company culture survey. I am sure that you will find many uses for them in your company to improve performance, morale and your bottom line. For additional information on how you can try and use assessments like these, please see the Appendix.

ANDREA ADAMS-MILLER

About the Author

Andrea Adams-Miller, MS, CEO & Founder of IgniteYourRelationships.com, & AvonleaPublishingCompany.com, *"Ignites the Spark, Fire, and Passion in Business Relationships"* for Corporations, Entrepreneurs, and Organizations. A respected and highly sought-after business consultant, keynote speaker, 9-time author, and award-winning radio show host, Andrea reveals the secrets to create, retain, and sustain lucrative 'REAL' relationships with stakeholders. She shows you how to quickly and easily solidify loyalty with your clients, employees, partners, and vendors to achieve the business relationships you only dare to dream, desire, and deserve!

Andrea has appeared on print, radio and television, such as: *Time* Magazine, 20/20, ABC, CBS, NBC, FOX, PBS, and Business News Daily. She shared the stage with celebrity speakers Brian Tracy (Executive Trainer), Harv Eckert (Millionaire Mind), James Malinchak (ABC's Secret Millionaire), Jack Canfield (Chicken Soup for the Soul), Stedman Graham (PR Executive), and more...

More information about www.IgniteYourRelationships.com is on page 160.

Putting the Sizzle in Your Business Relationships

Create, Retain, & Sustain Lucrative REAL Relationships
with Your Clients, Employees, Partners, & Vendors

by Andrea Adams-Miller

Introduction
Put the REAL back in 'REAL'ationships for lucrative business success!
~ ANDREA ADAMS-MILLER

When it comes to successful, lucrative business relationships, research trends indicate that corporations who focus on building solid relationships excel over their competitors, especially in times of economic recession. However, the art of building solid relationships with clients, employees, partners and vendors, hereafter referred to as stakeholders, requires a niched skillset in order to be profitable. Many successful organizations have invested in various programs to facilitate these skillsets, including Dale Carnegie's *How to Win Friends & Influence People* and Stephen Covey's *The 7 Habits of Highly Effective People.* Yet corporations still seek that missing element from these trainings, the element of establishing profitable long-standing relationships with their stakeholders. Frankly, successful businesses know and rely on attracting the right contacts, stoking intimate customer connections and igniting long-term stakeholder loyalty.

As any astute business executive, you are probably wondering, "What are the secrets to prospecting for the right stakeholders, how do we convert these potential consumers to become repeat investors and how do we keep them loyal to invest again and again for the long term? To answer your questions, I will reveal some of the top secrets from my proprietary program, *Putting the Sizzle in Your Business Relationships*™ here in this chapter. Thank goodness, right? Because let's be honest, you and I both know that in tough times customers, employees, partners and vendors can be fickle when it comes to motivating them towards profitable loyalty. Even when the economy is strong, any smart business owner, executive staff member or salesperson knows that even faithful stakeholders can be unpredictable!

This stage of profitable loyalty is never reached if you or your team doesn't make connections with the right prospects. Profitable loyalty wanes when the stakeholders sense a slack in contact or if the stakeholders perceive (i.e., feel) your business no longer has consideration for their needs. Preventing this misperception of unfulfilled business cohesion and unfulfilled business needs is easy. Fortunately, these stakeholders can be transformed into **profitable loyalty stakeholders** when the secrets are applied. Maintaining solid relationships that foster perpetual business loyalty relies on three main factors: connection, contact, and consideration. These three factors are necessary to create, retain and sustain loyal long-term profitable business relationships.

The Value of Long-Term Relationships

Feelings ignored result in investments returned. ~ Andrea Adams-Miller

Previously, the word "feel" was mentioned as a replacement for perception, as in when a client feels there is a business communication breakdown.

Although at some point you may have heard, "There are no emotions in business," feelings cannot be denied as playing a major factor in our decision making process. Anyone in business any length of time will tell you that emotions are ever-present, albeit often repressed or shown as anger or frustration. Some company executives do not believe in vesting in "feelings" when it comes to business. However, the fact remains that it is people who run and are employed by businesses, and those same people base their buying or investing habits on emotions, also known as feelings. To not address their "feelings" results in business suicide. Most business people cannot maintain long-term, healthy business relationships if they are not willing to take into consideration the people behind the business. If their feelings are negated or overlooked, they will show their displeasure by shopping or investing elsewhere. They will likely not reinvest or return, regardless of what damage control tactics are used. To be blunt, most people buy or invest based on their emotions more often than they buy or invest with their calculators.

To put this into dollars and cents, according to SCORE (2003), the cost of building a relationship with a new client is five times higher than keeping the client already on your roster. If those figures aren't compelling enough, consider the financial loss of turnover within the staff. In a meta-analysis by Sasha Corp (2007), the loss of a long-term relationship with an employee can cost from 25% to 100% of that former employee's annual wage in order to secure their replacement. The more specialized training involved, the higher the cost associated with recruiting, training and placement. Additionally, there will likely be loss of income when dissolving business relationships, and there will likely be an increase in legal expenses when dissolving business partnerships. Regardless of its level, each business relationship is extremely valuable in time and other resources, let alone the uncertainty that a replacement will be as good as expected.

This means that the value of keeping these current relationships with clients, employees, partners and vendors is much greater fiscally than ever before considering the recent economy. For example, consider the advantage of keeping one employee for an average of 20 years. Research shows that longevity prevents up to 10, 20 or more turnovers in a 20-year span. Furthermore, it is imperative to avoid the deterioration of other business relationships as a side effect. As one relationship dissolves, the trickle-down effect of discord or absence of one person or business may negatively affect the progression of business and/or the cohesiveness of the surviving team. Breakdown of the core team often results in additional business losses in which many companies are unable to survive, let alone thrive.

Considering the value of a business relationship, employers are becoming more mindful of the value of "feelings." Identifying and assessing feelings increases as a priority once businesses realize the financial gains and losses connected with NOT being emotionally intelligent. Try as we might to avoid emotions in business, research reveals that even educated, experienced and intelligent business people buy and invest based on their gut feelings, although they convince themselves they have taken into account a multitude of other factors that make their decisions educated or informed. Call it what they want, the fact remains that emotions cannot be discounted. To gain a better understanding of clients' perceptions, expectations, reactions and processes results in the need for greater emotional intelligence, also known as emotional quotient (EQ).

The Value of Emotional Intelligence

The more you show off your emotional intelligence (EQ), the more your customer loyalty persists. The more you show off your cognitive intelligence (IQ), the more your customer loyalty resists. ~ Andrea Adams-Miller

Emotional Intelligence (EQ) is the skillset of learning how different people respond emotionally to varying management styles and personality styles in the moment of a particular situation. Whereas one client or employee may be motivated to excel or invest by competition and criticism, another stakeholder will be turned off and rescind repeat investment with the company or products. It is imperative for all staff members dealing with stakeholders to learn how to read the emotional responses of others and respond accordingly. Emotional intelligence, once considered not applicable to business, has become increasingly prevalent in the business world.

Up to 75% of Fortune 500 companies are getting on board with emotional intelligence training. The financial success in accounting for the emotions of others while considering your own emotions has been found to increase the sustainability of business relationships. Not only is EQ financially sustainable for businesses, research reveals that the highest producers in a company rate the highest on emotional intelligence. Furthermore, these highest producers tend to earn over $29,000 a year more than their less emotionally intelligent peers! When it comes to retention, sales and customer recruitment, emotionally intelligent communication is the key.

Fortunately, those not blessed with natural EQ skills can learn them. Even professionals with natural ability or previous training excel the more often they practice these abilities and take courses that refresh their skills. When igniting the spark, fire and passion in relationships, take into account that it is important to bring in an outside consultant to point out where business relationship quality is lacking. One of the greatest gifts for which clients thank me is coming to them as an outsider to critique departments and employees utilizing my own EQ skills. In using EQ skills in conjunction with the feedback, the staff is open to suggestions and actually welcomes the critiques. Furthermore, when you finally make that decision to invest in your business relationship by seeking a consultant, it needs to be an experienced professional who can do more than assess and identify the issues. This consultant needs to be able to demonstrate the actions to take to increase the relationships in various situations, such as what we do at IgniteYourRelationships.com. To make sure your company is hiring the right professionals, please download the EQ consultant checklist at www.IgniteYourRelationships.com/EQConsultationChecklist.

Strategies from the World of Interpersonal Relationships
Business relationships parallel personal relationships. How you behave at home could end in divorce. How you behave at work could get you fired. Either way, you're out! ~ Andrea Adams-Miller

Speaking of emotional intelligence, any business professional would be amiss to think that successful relationships don't parallel personal relationships. In fact, after decades of success in the interpersonal world of relationships, I noticed my clients came to me time and time again with issues and problems that were directly related to the workplace which directly affected their personal lives. In order to be of assistance, I started offering a few minutes of our consultation sessions focused on their businesses. Interestingly enough, the successful advice I gave for their business relationships were based on the years of research and experience I had with interpersonal relationship issues. Intrigued clients were pleased with the analogies I used comparing business relationships to those in their personal lives because they said my analogies made them "get it" and understand the relationship situations at work in a different light. My reputation for business success became more widely known, to the extent that eventually, business professionals were asking for appointments solely for their business relationships.

With my success both in business and in interpersonal relationships, I became known in the media as "the leading international authority on healthy relationships both in business and in the bedroom," a surprisingly catchy phrase, yet amazingly accurate. Please understand, I offer this background story not to brag, but so you understand where I am coming from professionally and so you understand the connections I have made between the two consulting businesses. My secrets for the business world are literally adaptations of my years of research and experience with interpersonal relationships focused on analogies comparing business to dating, relationships and sexuality! While this may seem bizarre, corporate leaders have told me they really appreciate it for several reasons. First of all, they say the stories I tell directly parallel situations at work that are realistic, easily understood and easily applicable to their organizations. Secondly, the juxtaposition between personal and professional relationships adds an edge that gets their staff excited about the trainings and programs I offer, generating a buzz like no other!

Another reason I share this information with you is because I believe that you can't really believe me until you know me, so it is equally important that I establish a great relationship with my audience. Only then will my messages be heard and my secrets applied to your organization. Lastly, I share this information to boost your confidence in following the secrets from my program *Putting the Sizzle in Your Business Relationships*™. Now that you know me, and now that you know I have the background, knowledge and experience to generate lucrative success when it comes to business relationships, you can receive the messages more effectively.

Connection is Key for Prospecting

Connection with the wrong prospects can lead to success, but connection with the RIGHT prospects is success! ~ Andrea Adams-Miller

The first step in building relationships is the recruitment of customers, also known as prospecting. The ability to connect with profitable prospects is best obtained when the staff seeks out the best prospects in the first place. Often, businessmen and businesswomen fail to identify who the best client is for their business. Additionally, these professionals work really hard at securing a prospect that is not necessarily the best fit. Painstakingly, they do everything they can to get this prospect to invest and try to hold onto that floundering client relationship. Then they struggle to keep that connection loyal year after year. This effort is exhausting and taxing in time, money and energy. To be honest, when you look at your return on investment (ROI) with this type of customer, the numbers don't support the effort. These are the clients that don't even make up the 60% of your breakeven point. Rather, they are what researchers refer to as the 20% that dips into your 80% profit margin!

To create new relationships with the appropriate clients, the company is responsible for designating someone to determine the ideal client for the business. This designee should be well versed in EQ and be able to determine the following questions: Who is this client? Where can this client be found? What does this client do at their work, at home and at their hobbies? Once this client pool is identified, then comes the task of making sure the business model/product being proposed matches the identified client pool. Often, at this step is where businesses make their biggest mistake by not hiring a business relationship consultant who understands the importance of securing the foundational demographics of their key prospects. What businesses may find is that without this core information they are trying to sell a product to a client who is not at the same level of need for the product, or the prospects are just not the right fit. If this foundation of prospects turns out to be truly the wrong fit, a business needs to do one of two things: 1) Get a new pool of prospects, or 2) Get a new product. It seems easier to start with the right information first.

Once these questions are answered and the product matches the client pool, then a business can begin the task of researching the proper events that attract their perfect client. Then the business needs to invest in sending their staff members to show up at these events where the perfect client is most likely to attend. These staffers can start creating relationships with the new prospects they meet by "dating" the appropriate people who fit the demographics of the perfect client. Again, not every professional is naturally skilled in networking at these events. Investing in consulting and mentoring to show your staff the best practices for maximizing these events is one of the most profitable moves a company can do for their future success. Although the analogy of dating may seem odd to use in business, recall that as a professional relationship consultant I have years of research and experience in the secrets of interpersonal success and how they parallel successful business relationships. Without this kind of dating, a business may be investing with the wrong people who are not a fit for a long-term relationship. Dating allows businesses the opportunity to weed out the type of 20% profitable clients from the 20% client pool that is draining the company budget! Too many businesses jump into a relationship *thinking* they have found the perfect partner when they haven't properly invested the time to *know* beyond a reasonable doubt that this new client is worth their investment.

Romancing the Contract
Asking someone to commit to you, whether it be marriage or a business contract, shouldn't be taken lightly, not by them and certainly not by you!
~ Andrea Adams-Miller

Once a business starts courting the right client, eventually it becomes obvious that the next step is to offer the business proposal. Again, this is where emotional intelligence comes in. If you wait too long to ask for the sale, it is possible another suitor is wooing your perfect client and by the time you pop the question it is too late! If the person is asked too soon for the sale, then there may be an automatic "no" just for assuming the "yes!" Assessing what the business client needs in order to make that next move is what becomes necessary at this point. In order to make your next move, the amount of contact becomes most important. Continued contact can be defined as face-to-face meetings, cards, emails, gifts, calls, etc. These traditional means of contact combined with special treatment such as the incorporation of nicknames or the sharing of insider information make the client more connected with the business. This continued regular contact, if only just to check in with the stakeholder, generates loyalty as it promotes a sense of nurturing which is essential to the client relationship. With regular contact and with asking the right questions of the client, the sales staff will gain valuable information that cues them into qualifying the proposal, qualifying the sale or qualifying the signing of the contract. In other words, once the client has qualified, the proposal, engagement and legal documentation for marriage are a done deal. Wedding bells are in your future and you are usually safe to order the celebratory cake!

Avoiding Business Infidelity
If you can't fulfill their needs, then someone else just might! ~Andrea Adams-Miller

Unfortunately, many businesses stop there with the done deal and this is where the trouble in a business marriage starts to brew. Like any honeymoon period, your client views you as their partner that can do no wrong, then they make excuses for what they consider your businesses misbehavior. Tempers quickly rise and the honeymoon period is over. Buyer's remorse sets in and the client is wondering what ever attracted them to you in the first place. When a stakeholder reaches this level of disconnect, your business is subject to *"Business Infidelity."*

All of a sudden any other competing business attracting attention starts looking pretty hot. Literally, your business may lose stakeholders to the very first competitor with the best marketing or the best gimmick that reflects the business needs of this consumer, collaborator, or investor. These frustrated businesses are looking to get their needs fulfilled; needs that they seemingly didn't get fulfilled from your organization. This is a situation any smart business owner or CEO recognizes as a threat to their business, a threat to their business relationships and a threat to their business's bottom line.

This is when many companies finally seek outside business relationship consulting, which is often a real struggle and sometimes just too late. It is so much more effective to have business relationship consulting *before* the problems fester, and even better to have the consulting prior to entering into more business relationships in the first place. While I can give you some of the top secrets from my program that have worked for past and present clients, please understand these suggestions are generalized, not tailored to your business, your staff and your clients. They may not be as successful as when you have the specialized consulting or training from *Putting the Sizzle in Your Business Relationships*™ program.

The best way to avoid business infidelity is by investing time and energy into your new partner above and beyond what they expect. Gifting them special bonuses, access to after-hours phone calls, private email access and special subscriptions to news tips are a few ways to make your new partner feel special and important. However, spreading out these gifts over time and giving them independent of birthdays and holidays will make them feel even more special. Of course, I am not suggesting you forget birthdays and holidays, but I am asking you to go the extra mile where your competition does not! For example, consider how special you feel when you get a hand addressed holiday card that is personally signed compared to the pre-addressed envelope with the fabricated message and pre-stamped signature. If you are like the hundreds of clients I have surveyed, you would know that the extra effort put into hand addressing and signing goes farther than ever expected. This is just one example of extra attention to detail. Remember that the extra attention to detail doesn't have to be expensive, but it does have to be well thought out and genuine. When you have achieved that ability, you have captured the essence of a real business relationship that can seemingly last forever.

Stroking the Business Erogenous Zone
Relationships are like coals, eventually they all end up a steady smolder;
all you have to do to reignite them is fan them a little to fuel up the flames.
~ Andrea Adams-Miller

Although you have achieved the level of sustainable competitive advantage in your business relationships by obtaining long-term relationships, remember that relationships in business ebb and flow just as they do in interpersonal relationships. To keep the fires stoked year after year, and to keep your clients hot for your business and your products, you need to seek ways to continually stroke their business erogenous zones!

The best ways to find these zones is to go back to basics. Research those first cues into your clients', employees', partners' and vendors' personas. What do they like, want or desire for themselves professionally and personally? Recall the little things they said all through your relationship and dating experiences. Hopefully you were writing them all down for later retrieval because this is where you really keep them coming back year after year.

For example, imagine late one night you see an infomercial on fishing lures and you recall your stakeholder has a fondness for fishing. You might even have recalled him/her mentioning the desire to retire, own a fishing boat and spend his/her days just casting that line. Imagine how much your client would love you if you sent them this lure with a message stating, *"Saw this fishing lure and I couldn't help but think of you! Not only did it get me thinking of your dream of fishing, it got me thinking that we might just have the perfect solution to get you there faster! We expect a whale of a fishing story and will call you next week to follow up! Happy fishing!"* Can you imagine this businessperson's pleasure at such a gift, an investment in their future happiness and success? Now this is the kind of secret that really keeps the fires stoked year after year!

From Red Hot to White Heat
The only way to change your relationships with others is to change yourself; put the sizzle back in your business relationships by investing in your business! ~ Andrea Adams-Miller

As you can see, business relationships are much more complicated than we realize. Although relationships take time, energy and money, when the right relationships are started through "*dating*" the right prospect, the effort is worth the investment. Plus, it is so much easier to step into the committed relationship when you have the emotional intelligence and the skillset to turn this informal relationship into a "*business marriage*". Finally, keeping a long-term relationship solid year after year takes more than just being there for them when they need something! It takes preventative planning before problems arise!

Recall that some of the best long-lasting relationships invested in premarital counseling before they got married! We all know we cannot change others; we can only change ourselves, so invest in your business and you'll see your business relationships can change for the better. Every company, no matter how well versed, no matter how successful, requires the secrets to maintain solid business relationships. Invest in yourself and your business relationships now and start utilizing the strategies to ignite the spark, fire and passion with your clients, employees, partners and vendors. Start today to facilitate profitable LOYALTY as you create, retain and sustain successful lucrative REAL business relationships!

KLAUS KOKOTT

About the Author

Klaus Kokott is a Managing Partner at Kokott, Wood & Associates, Inc. An exceptional domestic and international retail career executive with a 25 year track record, Klaus provides deep insight into the skills and aptitudes employment candidates need to be successful.

Klaus Kokott held positions from accounting to VP of Sales & Marketing at Fortune 50 companies. He managed or worked with professionals in every departmental category. He deploys this functional understanding to drive home the importance of interdependent roles. He has consulted to multi-national retail organizations producing successful collaboration between diverse groups and departments resulting in increased sales, market share and profitability.

His executive roles serve retail operations, marketing, sales, project management, strategic planning and implementation, succession planning, market expansion, and logistics.

More information about Kokott, Wood & Associates, LLC. is on page 162.

Hire for Fit versus Hire for Fill

by Klaus Kokott

Employee turnover, and more importantly executive turnover, significantly impacts a company's ability to excel. Even a strong and stable leader at the helm can only do so much, and a company's products and services will only take them so far. True success and excellence come from a strong dynamic team—one built on similar beliefs, strong ethical values and behaviors that mirror and complement the overall company culture—not one built on *gut feel* hiring decisions. This chapter will provide you with the key components for *Hiring for Fit* versus simply *Hiring for Fill*. They include the following:

Preparing for an Effective Search

- The rationale behind the effort.
- The importance of understanding the company's culture.
- Identifying the key elements of the position to be "fitted".
- A discussion of the profile of an "ideal" candidate.

The Qualifying Process

- An overview of what an extensive candidate qualification process should entail.
- The process and benefits of a formal presentation of candidate finalists.

Candidate Selection and On-Boarding Process

- The personal interviews conducted by the hiring authority.
- A discussion of the offer acceptance stage, and concluding with
- The on-boarding process of the successful candidate.

Rationale

According to studies conducted by The Booz Company, the 2011 CEO *forced* turnover rate was 2%, representing only 55 out of 2,500 of the world's top companies. When contrasted with the 110% hourly employee turnover rate, as reported by the National Restaurant Federation, that number seems almost miniscule. Even that seemingly small executive turnover rate significantly impacts a company's ability to thrive. It is in this context that *Hiring for Fit* rather than *Hiring for Fill* becomes especially important.

Each of these dynamic team qualities mentioned above—beliefs, values, and behaviors—must be identified and quantified during the qualification phase if the hiring process is to be successful. Omitting any single factor of the equation creates the potential for a *bad hire* and increased employee turnover. Only by utilizing a qualifying, interviewing and hiring process addressing each critical area can a company avoid *Hiring for Fill*.

With that basic groundwork laid, let's delve into the heart of the topic and how to *Hire for Fit*.

Company Culture

To begin with, *Company Culture*, as defined by BusinessDictionary.com, is composed of the values and behaviors that contribute to the unique social and psychological environment of an organization.

Even in today's market of high unemployment, the ability to present an attractive company culture is often a key element in persuading top-flight candidates to pursue a particular position. While prospective candidates are certainly interested in compensation, title, growth and location, their interest is piqued when the description of a company's culture *fits* their own. Aspects such as internal promotions, tenure, community involvement, and marketing tactics, among others in a wide assortment of traits, all translate into the creation of a company culture in the candidate's mind.

However, this is one of the most challenging topics for many executives to describe. If you were to ask this question of 100 executives, it's possible that less than 5% could provide an answer with accuracy *and* conviction. What sort of impression will this make on a perspective employee?

Defining the company culture is the very first step in the hiring process. Any candidate worth interviewing will ask this question of the internal or external recruiter enticing them to explore a particular position.

There are a number of ways to determine what a company's culture truly is. An internal management team can develop and participate in a number of exercises designed to identify the culture. The drawback is that these can be slanted by company politics. An unbiased third party consulting firm, skilled in developing and facilitating this process, can be hired to highlight what *it* determines the company culture to be. A third method, and perhaps the most truthful but also the most complicated, engages the customer in defining the culture. Depending on the situation's urgency, companies may have to combine the first and second alternatives, following up at a later date with customer input. Whatever the chosen method, this is something that *every* company should clearly and accurately define.

It's not our intent to describe the process of building a company culture, but rather simply to point out that it is important to candidates. The following list highlights some traits you may want to ensure are addressed in your company culture statement:

- Mission and vision clarity.
- Commitment to promoting internally.
- Fully empowered employees.
- Company principles, ethics and morals.
- Trusting relationships.
- Highly effective leadership.
- Effective and constantly improving systems and processes.
- Compensation and rewards based on performance.
- Customer-focused.
- Effective 180 and 360 communications.
- Demonstrated commitment to employees' continuous growth and learning.
- Track record that demonstrates hiring and retaining excellence.
- Flexibility to meet or exceed competition.
- Culture of accountability.
- Innovative and supportive of new ideas.

Key Elements of the Position and Position Description (tangible)

We have worked with clients whose reactions ranged from blank stares to rolling eyes when asked to provide a written position description. A key to recognizing this element's value is helping them overcome the notion that this is merely a necessary evil. It is a critical piece that helps identify candidates who will represent the company to the customer and will be charged with implementing the company's vision, strategy and action plans.

Who should be involved in developing the position description? Those who will be impacted by the candidate's work and results should be accountable for providing an accurate description. Based on our experience, this usually includes:

• Human Resources.
• The incumbent.
• Key interacting personnel, such as direct reports, managers and peers.
• Executive approval or executive committee review to ensure the job description fits within the company culture.

At a minimum, an effective position description should include the following tangible elements:

• The position's key objective.
• The roles and responsibilities of the job.
• The desired length of industry experience or experience in particular job functions.
• Any required or desirable education, training, or certifications.
• The desired personal and professional characteristics or qualities.
• The general reporting structure.
• Some general description of possible career paths.

Most companies have position descriptions of some sort. The important factors to consider are whether or not these documents accurately describe the job in its present form and outline the expectations.

Ideally, a periodic review of each position description is conducted around the time performance appraisals are reviewed. This is an excellent time to compare actual job functions versus what is pre-printed on the evaluation form. Another review opportunity is at the time of decision to fill the vacant position. If the slot is vacant due to termination or resignation, it's a good idea to assess if the expectations varied from the position description. Generally, this is a collaborative effort between the hiring team and the recruiter, whether internal or external.

Profile of the Ideal Candidate (intangible)

While the position description should provide the basis for highlighting key tangible aspects of a candidate's background, it's not possible to identify the ideal candidate without first determining if his or her intangibles match those of the management team. In this case, we're referring to the team of peers and managers. Keep in mind that "match" is a relative term. Can the parties work together because the intangibles are complementary or will they struggle to gel?

This is an extremely important but frequently overlooked aspect of identifying and qualifying the best candidates for a particular position. A candidate should meet all or most of the qualifications set forth in the position description. However, what are the other desirable traits that the "*ideal*" candidate would exhibit? How will the candidate fit in with the existing management team? What is the candidate's management style? Is the candidate a leader or follower, aggressive or laid back? Do the short and long-range goals for personal development and advancement match the opportunity or the company's offerings? In the end, the desirable intangibles should not be based on the hiring manager's personal opinions. They should be based on facts—the facts as derived from the components and profiles of the existing management team.

To say it is challenging to identify the desired intangibles without the benefit of a base profile and a clear understanding of the management team's own intangibles is an understatement. One of the tools we've embraced to help identify these traits is a bank of three different assessments designed to highlight a team's behaviors, motivation and thinking patterns. These assessments, provided by Pam Brooks, another contributor to this book, provide a very objective measure to a subjective process. It is from these assessments that we gain a clear understanding of how a company's management team functions, interacts and reacts to multiple business issues and pressures in conducting its daily business. Only after the company's intangibles are brought to light is it possible to develop a list of desirable traits in the ideal candidate. Without this critical step in the hiring process, approving a hire is much more likely to be based on gut instinct and hiring for fill than *Hiring for Fit.*

Qualifying of Potential Candidates

A solid candidate qualification process is the most important element in the hiring process. If not conducted in a controlled and systematic manner, the compromised process can lead to a disastrous hire. There are nine elements to effectively qualifying a candidate. Omitting any of them introduces an unacceptable level of risk, which could be very costly. To fully implement this process, the hiring team must be prepared to address each of the following elements:

- A positioning paper accurately describing the company's business, culture and management style.
- A detailed and effectively written position description.
- A listing of key elements required for the position.
- A list of subjective questions designed to highlight the traits of the ideal candidate.
- A written questionnaire that the candidate must complete, based on several factors including the position description, the position's key elements, ideal candidate questions, and specific questions based on points of interest in the candidate's resume. In our own firm, we call this a Skill SetMatch Qualification Questionnaire, normally consisting of 25-35 in-depth questions pertaining to the position, desired management skills and specific probing questions resulting from initial phone screening..
- Completion of each of the three assessments.
- Professional references.
- Background checks.
- Personal interview questions.

At this point, the process becomes a *go forward* or *dismiss* scenario. To continue, each candidate must satisfactorily complete each element or be removed from consideration. The following section explains the importance of some of these steps.

Positioning Paper

An effective *positioning paper* is not something you want to leave to chance. Given the critical need for consistency at the beginning of the qualifying process, this document will enable each team member involved in the interview process to confidently project the company's management style and line of business as it relates to the position and the culture. Nothing is left to chance or memory.

Key Elements

While the position description will clearly outline the job, the *list of key elements* of the job that the successful candidate must possess will help identify those traits and skills. It is important that the management team is in agreement regarding this list. During candidate discussions, it's important to probe for each of the elements, ensuring to take notes for future team discussions and overall candidate evaluation.

Questions of the Ideal Candidate

Having a written set of *ideal candidate questions* is very important, even if only for the purposes of consistency. Many hiring managers categorize these into nice-to-have and need-to-have. As noted earlier, these questions are based upon the information gained from the results of the three assessments of the management team. The candidate's responses, which should be in the form of actual examples resulting from competency-specific questioning, will provide initial insight into how the candidate may fit into the company and management team.

Assuming everyone in the process is satisfied that the position description accurately describes the opportunity at hand, each of the position's key elements should be identified separately so that the candidate can be questioned about their experience and abilities regarding each. Agreement on the key points is critical. Each candidate must be asked the same questions regarding these key points during the interview as this enables the future comparison between the various candidates' answers. Consistency is the key. Many of your interview questions will center on the key elements of the position, but there are many other areas of the candidate's background that will need to be explored as well. We'll cover those shortly.

Written Questionnaire

The purpose of a *written questionnaire*, which we call the *Skill SetMatch Qualification Questionnaire*, is to conduct an in depth probe of the candidate's background. This questionnaire is sent to a candidate only if the initial telephone interview produces a very strong candidate. Given the time commitment required of both the candidate and hiring team, it is a waste of everyone's time to administer this questionnaire if there are doubts about the candidate's qualifications after the initial screening.

This questionnaire should be developed prior to the initial telephone interviews or screening calls. These objective questions, many of which are competency-specific, require the candidate to explain their experiences, approaches and management style by providing relevant examples from their work history. In addition to these predetermined questions, which will be asked of all candidates, hiring managers and interviewers should have the opportunity to ask questions specifically geared towards the individual candidate and designed to elicit additional information based on a resume or responses to an interviewer's notes from prior discussions.

The purpose of this qualification step is to provide the candidate the opportunity to respond to interview questions in a more relaxed environment and to be able to write in-depth, thoughtful and meaningful answers. Frequently, candidates will review the questions, give themselves time to collect their thoughts and notes and then begin writing responses one to two days later.

The quality of the written responses will enable the reader to ascertain not only the relevant experience level, but also the candidate's written communication style and thinking process. As recruiters, we also consider the candidate's timeliness and completeness of responses as interest level indicators. Other indicators include the candidate's attention to detail with regards to spelling, grammar, punctuation and response consistency.

Candidate Assessments

The series of three *candidate assessments* are only given to candidates who have successfully completed each phase of the qualification process to this point. In addition to describing the candidate's management style, these assessments determine if the candidate will fit with the management team. They also suggest specific lines of questioning to help uncover particular strengths and possible weaknesses. They become a tool that can pinpoint these prior to a candidate's first day on the job.

Our firm selects the top five to eight candidates, based on the overall quality of the verbal screening process and the written questionnaires, to move forward with the set of assessments.

The management team can now compare the candidate assessments to the management team's assessments.

Reference Checks

The value of *reference checks* can not be overstated. While many employment offers are extended on the condition of favorable reference checks, we conduct these well in advance of a personal interview with the hiring manager. The evaluation process involved in reference checks actually starts when the list is requested of the candidate. It's important to consider how quickly that list was provided, the management level of the professional references, as well as the relevancy of the references. When a strong list is quickly provided, it usually indicates the candidate's career search is serious. On the other hand, providing references who would normally only be viewed as associates, business contacts or vendors of previous employers may indicate problems at the last place of employment. Personal references are not taken into consideration. Written references carry more significance when signed and dated by a candidate's superior, with contact information included.

As a way to ensure accuracy and candid responses, we utilize a process involving anonymous responses to a series of online questions provided by seven total references: two managers, three peers, and two direct reports. The responses are then scored to provide an overall professional reference rating.

Background Checks

Equally as vital are *background checks*. As with reference checks, background checks should be conducted prior to a personal interview. Most candidates expect to have a background check conducted, but the level of detail is important. Our firm conducts background checks for the following:
- Criminal at the federal, state and local levels.
- Driving record.
- Credit score.
- Education verification.

Given the detail of these checks, it has been our experience to advise candidates of our process at the outset and provide them with an opportunity to explain the information that may be uncovered. If an issue exists and the candidate discloses it, we can make a preliminary determination as to how it may impact the qualification process. On the other hand, failure to disclose an issue until after it's uncovered in the background check calls the candidate's judgment into question.

Personal Interview Questions

The *personal interview* is usually the final phase of the candidate's qualifying process. Although technologies such as Skype and traditional video conferencing have made some inroads into the process, especially in cases of extreme urgency or exceptionally remote locations, this should be a face-to-face interview.

As the hiring team will usually interview the top three to five candidates in a *round robin* format, consistency again plays a key role in identifying the candidate with the best fit. A set of situational questions is used for each candidate, with flexibility allowed for questioning into areas identified by the assessments. Personal interviews we conduct, with the client present, usually contain 25 to 35 questions.

In addition to evaluating the candidate's responses, there are a number of other interview characteristics that may provide clues as to the candidate's ability and comfort level to take on the role. Was the candidate too quick or take a normal amount of time to consider a comprehensive response? Did the interviewer have to repeat questions in different formats in order to elicit responses? Did the candidate provide actual examples or theoretical responses to competency- specific questions? Did the candidate ask strong follow up questions? Did the candidate's use of industry vernacular and terminology seem commensurate with the management level of the position?

Presentation of Final Candidates

This is a step many internal and external recruiters choose to omit, but our experience shows that the organized presentation of finalists in a format enabling the hiring team to compare strengths and similarities to their own team profile leads to excellent discussions about the candidates and moves the process along in a decisive manner.

Our firm produces a *Candidate Presentation and Interview Guide*, which is mailed to the client approximately one week prior to our final meeting with them. This manual provides the client with a very thorough understanding of the candidates' capabilities, how they will fit within the management team, and the most effective way to manage each candidate to ensure peak performance. During our final visit, we openly share our feedback and impressions about each candidate based on the correspondence, discussions, and information we've gathered during the qualifying process.

The guide is also used during the final interview process, sharing insights into candidates' modus operandi and laying the groundwork for excellent probing questions. As all finalists' information is included in one packet, it fosters a more focused approach on management's part to move the selection process along. Too often, hiring managers are provided resumes on a *first come first served* basis, making candidate comparisons challenging. This can also result in the dismissal of qualified candidates whose only fault was having their resume on the hiring manager's desk too soon in the process.

Final Personal Interview with Hiring Authority

Once the hiring authority has had time to review and digest the candidates presented, personal interviews are scheduled. The *Candidate Presentation and Interview Guide* should be the basis for the interview. Having reviewed each candidate's information in detail, making notes as to areas of interest and follow up questions, the interviewers will be thoroughly prepared for an in depth conversation and interview. Additionally, we will have provided assessment-based guidance with regards to further exploring the intangibles needed to create a solid fit with the management team. Based on our experience, this culmination of the qualifying process, in depth information, comparisons, and interviews leads to a final decision.

Offer Extension and Acceptance

The work is done. Candidates have been interviewed. A decision has been made. This is precisely the time to pay special attention to details! The offer should be straightforward and contain no elements of surprise for either party. From the recruiter's standpoint, topics such as compensation, benefits, relocation, work environment, special requirements, etc. should have been covered at the outset of the qualifying process. Regardless of who is conducting the search, qualified candidates should be *trial closed* several times along the way. Ignoring this step could lead to embarrassment and disappointment on both sides at the very time congratulations should be in order.

Our experience indicates that an initial offer should be extended verbally by the recruiter, whether internal or external. This allows for both parties to ask questions in a buffered setting and provides for an offer to be tweaked, if necessary, prior to its presentation in writing. After the verbal offer's acceptance, a final written offer is presented to the candidate for signature. The final offer should not contain any surprises whatsoever and should be signed by the candidate within the agreed upon time frame.

On-Broading Process

Having just committed to a major long- term investment of salary, benefits, and perhaps relocation, the company must have a plan in place for the proper on-boarding of any new employee. In principle, this is similar to any plan for the justification, implementation and full utilization of a fixed asset.

This plan should begin with the customary completion of HR forms and personal introductions, but then progress to meetings with the immediate manager, pertinent members of the management team, and peers. Along the way, the new employee is verbally provided with direction and expectations. From there the new employee should be provided with a more formal 90-day plan that will chart progress and objectives. Naturally, this will vary in complexity based on the nature of the position. The key point is to create a clear understanding of the objectives. It's always better to be in line with these during the *honeymoon* phase.

Conclusion

We hope we've provided some valuable information, context and insight into the process of *Hiring for Fit*. It's a detailed and comprehensive approach that takes real time and effort to implement, but following the process is the best way for your company to ensure it will hire only the best people. And that is a goal worth pursuing at any company.

DEBRA ZIMMER

About the Author

Debra Zimmer, MBA & Founder of The Expert Marketing Coach is an experienced marketing executive. After 15 years of growing entrepreneurial businesses at companies such as Microsoft, where she attracted 700,000 customers into an online community in 18 months—and then launched a second one and grew it to 250,000 members in 10 months, Debra Zimmer struck out on her own to grow an online retail store to 6-figures of income and put it on autopilot for three years. With an engineering degree and an MBA from Columbia Business School, Debra is the undisputed authority in helping experts, entrepreneurs and executives to focus their brilliance and magnify their impact. She now teaches her proprietary marketing systems to private clients and groups worldwide.

Debra is a Certified Executive Mastermind Coach, a Certified Inbound Marketer and the coauthor of *Lessons from the Recession*.

More information about The Expert Marketing Coach is on page 164.

The Business Case for Social Media

3 Ways to Engage Your Team and Grow Your Brand

by Debra Zimmer

I n this new social society where your customers, your workforce and your prospective employees all have instant access to their own personal social media megaphone, many of you are struggling to control your corporate image. You fear what to do with disgruntled employees whose public ranting gets picked up by the press. Your executives inadvertently hide behind closed doors not knowing how to meld their personal opinions with your organization image. You have employees who are distracted by social media, which results in reduced productivity. But banning social media during business hours just doesn't work.

It can feel impossible to control. It can become frustrating when it feels like no one is paying attention or following "no-post" rules. It can be overwhelming to figure out how to reign it all in.

This chapter is for business leaders who are frustrated and confused by social media and tired of trying to contain and restrain employee engagement. Holding employees back isn't working. Yet how do you let them loose without sabotaging the efforts of marketing and public relations? How do you use your human capital to enhance your brand and develop your employees while increasing their commitment to the organization? And how can you attract more highly qualified candidates in the process?

By *embracing* the changes this new social society brings, you can harness the power of social media to elevate your organization, employees and executives to new levels of engagement, attracting more customers and qualified employees at the same time.

I'm going to give you a clear understanding of the business case for embracing the use of social media by your executives, managers AND employees. I will outline why and how to leverage your human capital to communicate your organizational values and your culture and reinforce your brand. This empowers your employees, improves retention and attracts highly qualified candidates into your business.

This information is designed for Executives, Managers, Marketing Professionals, HR Professionals, Team leaders, or anyone that wants a better understanding of how to position themselves or their employees as an expert, industry leader, or successful professional.

First, you will discover why giving your executives a public face on social media can benefit both the business (via hiring, retention and growth) AND your executives. Second, you'll discover how to encourage your employees to create and promote their personal brand on social media (and how this leads to business growth). Third, you'll also learn how to create a social media policy that increases retention and attracts more highly qualified job candidates.

To begin with, let's look at why executive participation on social media is so important. Did you know that only 16% of all CEOs in the United States are using social media to communicate with customers? Would it surprise you to know that CEOs themselves expect that number to balloon to 57% within 3-5 years? [1]

Why is the number of CEO's embracing social networks about to explode? Let's look at the data.

Research shows that 82% of people are **more likely to trust** a company whose CEO and leadership team engage with social media AND 77% are **more likely to buy** from a company whose values and mission are defined through CEO and executive leadership participation on social media.[2]

A separate survey by Brand Fog shows an impressive 51% of Facebook fans and 67% of Twitter followers are **more likely to buy** the brands they follow or of which they are fans.[3] Because people like to follow other people more than they like to follow faceless companies, your executive participation on social media can enhance engagement, communication and trust among followers, which leads to major implications on customer purchase decisions. In short,

$$CEO + SM = \$.$$

You can see why giving your executives a public face on social media can benefit both the business AND your executives. First, your organization gains an increase in trust in the leadership, the brand and the organization. It humanizes the organization, enabling a deeper connection or bond than is possible with a faceless entity.

The executive gains trust from employees, partners and customers. They become more effective communicators, are more accessible and become more trustworthy. The executive is able to build his personal brand and share his personal mission while furthering the corporate mission. When people know what your executive stands for, it helps him or her attract key partners, customers and employees. It's a win-win.

This is scary for some executives because to be effective on social media, one must also become vulnerable. The executive becomes more exposed. The risks go up, but so do the rewards. Fear of sharing the wrong information and fear that their mistakes will be magnified are some of the reasons why 70.3% of Fortune 500 CEO's have no presence on social networks at all.[4]

However, according to an IBM study, "in order to effectively lead a company, management competencies will have to be reinvented around a new set of principles including transparency, integrity, collaboration, and consistent communication with stakeholders about company vision, mission, and values through social media channels."[5] Outperforming organizations have a 30% higher emphasis on this type of openness than average companies.[6]

To create an outperforming organization, CEO's are differentiating their organizations through new and deeper connections that include two key initiatives: **empowering employees through values** and **engaging customers as individuals**. Social Media plays an integral role in both of these initiatives.

When it comes to empowering employees there is currently a disconnect between what executives perceive is the issue and what employees want. According to Deloitte's new "Core Values and Beliefs" survey, executives rank competitive compensation (62%) and financial performance (65%) among the top factors influencing culture on the job. However, employees say the intangibles—regular and candid communication (50%) and access to management (47%)—outweigh the tangibles of compensation (33%) and financial performance (24%).[7] This simply means that executives are disconnected from what employees value the most, which is open communication and access to management.

To bridge the gap and improve workplace culture, executives need to open up communication and be more accessible. The good news is that social networking is probably the best tool available to improve communication and access to management. Executives that embrace social media as a means for open communication create a more collaborative culture, which is a necessity for future success. When this happens, employees are then encouraged to speak up, connect with collaborators and innovate.

In this open, collaborative culture where formal controls have loosened, there is an increased need for organizational values and a clear sense of purpose to guide decisions and actions. Social media facilitates this open, collaborative culture. It also increases the organization's vulnerability because any employee interaction on social networks, whether positive or negative, can become the next primetime news story instantly. In order to reduce this vulnerability in the new open workplace, employees need to embody the organization's values and mission and undergo training, similar to how executives undergo media training before talking with the press.

This brings us to the second point, which is why you want to encourage your employees to create and promote their personal brand on social media (and how this leads to business growth).

Employees will also need a new set of skills and tools to be collaborative, communicative and creative, which may require some simple training. Having a diverse and extensive network of contacts will give employees access to potential collaborators, prospective customers and prospective employees. Access to the employees' network will benefit the organization by increasing its reach in attracting more qualified employees, customers and collaborators.

Similarly, the executive team will also need to look at their social networks as an asset portfolio. The IBM 2012 CEO study concludes, "To lead in unfamiliar territory amid constant change, CEOs will need to learn from their own networks. They will need to assemble those networks like portfolios—with generational, geographic, institutional diversity. Then, they'll need to help their organizations do the same." To do this, executives will need assistance in overcoming their fears of social media, such as being overwhelmed, not having the time, being too unfamiliar, fearing the commitment and feeling too old.[8] This can be accomplished with training, a personal social media plan and, in some cases, a social media manager.

Transforming your team into social executives also supports recruiting efforts as "78% of respondents would prefer to work for a company whose leadership is active on social media."[9] Likewise, when employees are active on social media and exemplify the values of the organization, their presence within their networks helps attract highly qualified prospective employees, customers and partners into the fold.

Let's take a minute to review what the data we've discussed shows us.

1. Having a CEO active on social media increases trust, which is directly measurable to an increase in likelihood to purchase.
2. People prefer to work for an organization whose leadership is active on social media.
3. Employees are more engaged and empowered when they receive regular and candid communication from and have access to management through social media channels.
4. Outperforming organizations have transparency, integrity, collaboration and consistent communication with employees, customers and partners about organization vision, mission, and values through social media channels.

How do you translate these findings into an effective social media implementation for your organization? There are 5 steps: 1) First is establishing a social media policy that is 2) aligned with the organization mission and values and embodied throughout the organization. 3) Next you need a social media plan for the organization as a whole. 4) Then your Executives need their own individual social media plan along with training. 5) Finally, your employees need a social media plan and training.

I told you I would teach you how to create a social media policy that increases retention and attracts more highly qualified job candidates, and now is that time. A social media policy doesn't need to be complex. It should include some elements like which employees can or cannot use social media as an official representative of the organization. Only a few employees, such as your executive or social media team, will be acting on an official basis as a representative of the organization. Most of your employees will be acting as themselves in a non-official capacity, and that will need to be covered in the guidelines too. In the appendix I've included directions for where you can get more articles on crafting a social media policy and download instructions for creating your own. I also provide a sample social media policy that can be created using a tool called The Social Media Policy Tool.

You'll notice that the sample social media policy includes topics such as "don't tell secrets" and "protect your own privacy," "be honest" and "respect copyright laws." This is also where you tell employees to respect the boundaries and confidentiality with their audience, organization, coworkers, customers, business partners and suppliers. When they find themselves in the middle of a controversy, they should stick to the facts and be the first to respond to their own mistakes. They need to think in advance about the possible consequences of their words. And, when possible, use a disclaimer.

A social media policy is something that should be reviewed with each employee individually or during social media training. Each employee should commit to the policy. Dianne Crampton's chapter refers to a process for rapid adoption of change. Driving the adoption of a new social media policy and open communication is a perfect example of how this process can be applied.

Once you've outlined what is acceptable Social Media behavior for your organization and its employees, you will want to discuss your corporate mission and values.

Your executives will lead by example on social media by embracing the organization's mission and values in their communication strategy. By reflecting the mission and values, they will drive adoption of the organization's culture among employees who use social networks to follow them or communicate with them. It will attract prospective employees who already embrace these values. It will also attract customers who value these traits and want to do business with like-minded people. Executive communications reflecting these values can also open opportunities with new strategic partners.

Your employees should know and internalize the organization's mission and values. An employee training should include a discussion as to how these values may be expressed on social networks along with a conversation of inappropriate behaviors. As employees mimic these business values, they too will attract prospective employees, customers and partners.

The next step in transitioning to a social organization is to create a social media plan for the organization. Social Media is not simply a function of marketing. It affects the whole organization, including sales, workforce engagement, customer support, IT and even internal collaboration functions.

The external and internal functions in the organization should have a social media plan to guide them. This social media plan should be based on The 5B's of Social Media™: Brand, Befriend, Broadcast, Buzz and Buy. The 5B's create a strategic framework upon which to base your social media initiatives. This same framework can be used to design training for the executive as well as the individual.

The 5B's of Social Media™

Let's take a look at what The 5B's of Social Media™ are and how they are applied.

"Brand" represents the need for a Brand strategy and a consistent representation across your social presence. Brand is where you define the main messages which the organization or individual stands for and how you want to be seen by the world. From an organization perspective, this is often decided at the corporate communications level. For each product or service offered, Brand is often managed by the Brand or product manager.

When it comes to the executive or even the individual employee, branding is often overlooked. But an executive needs to pay attention to his/her brand as well, especially any individual who will act as an official representative of the organization. A simple process can walk the executive or representative through the act of establishing their own personal objectives overlaid with those of their official role. Even employees benefit from this training as it helps them think about what they stand for, how they want to be viewed by the world and how their behavior can affect future employment opportunities. Everyone gains by taking the time to think about their "Brand" in advance.

An executive's or spokesperson's brand will need to reflect both the organization and individual. In the appendix is an example of Michael Rapino's social media networks. He is the CEO of LiveNation and one of the most active Fortune 500 CEOs on twitter. His Twitter handle is @rapino99. He mostly tweets about the entertainment industry, which is his company's primary business. He follows other entertainment industry executives, musicians, industry writers, analysts and business news sources. His followers include these and many entertainment industry fans. His image is that of a public representative of the company.

While his twitter presence reflects how one can use social media to engage partners, clients and customers, his branding stops there. If you look at any other profile of his on social media, the branding is inconsistent or non-existent. His Facebook profile image successfully bridges the world of personal and professional personas, but he fails to utilize the network for communication and relationship building with the public in a way that he achieves on twitter. His LinkedIn presence is non-existent. His PR team hasn't even provided a photo to Forbes. To be most effective, one's branding needs to be consistent across social media platforms.

The second phase of a social media plan is to "Befriend" or grow your network. Studies show that having a broad and diverse network increases the value of a network. "Befriend" is the phase where you are deliberately growing your network and introducing yourself to possible future collaborators. Social Media is a tool that facilitates the growth and connectivity of such a network.

The easiest relationships to build on social media are with people who already know, like and trust you. That's where you start. Then you meet new people by leveraging your relationship with the people who already know, like and trust you.

Let me give you an example of the value of networking which directly transfers to social media. I'm a graduate of Columbia Business School and attend alumni meetings in Denver. One meeting was held in the home of a fellow alumnus who is a VP of an international cable TV corporation. The conversation turned toward networking and he made a huge impression on me when he said, "That's why I go to The World Financial Summit. I don't go for the sessions, I go for the networking."

Surprised? I was. That's a man who lives by the value of networking. "I go to the World Financial Summit for the networking." Here's a man earns over $10 million dollars per year and he is consciously evaluating opportunities based on the potential value of the networking.

I'd like to point out a few errors that people make when it comes to their networking. First, he didn't say, "I only want to talk to people I know," which is what a lot of people do when they get on social media. They only want to talk with their immediate friends and family. Tight networks where you know everyone have been proven to be less effective than open networks where you have a lot of loose connections to people who run in different circles.

Second, he didn't even say the networking would have any immediate results. He knew that the whole purpose was that other world leaders would be there and therefore he should be there too. It wasn't whom he met that was important. It was that he was meeting someone who someday might know someone he wants to talk to. He's looking for people who understand how important their network is and the art of relationships and referrals.

Now you know why the IBM report concludes that executives of the future will need a broad and diverse network. And employees increase their value to prospective employers when they have a broad network. It works whether you are the CEO or the mailroom clerk.

Now, once you have your "Befriending" strategy in place, you will need to know how and when to craft messages to your network so your network begins working for you.

That leads us to the third success principle, "Broadcast." "Broadcast" is your approach to communications sent to your network, including the frequency and the content mix. The organization will have its overall content strategy, then each product or service will have its own plan for what it broadcasts to whom and when. Some of this content can be planned in advance (like tips, quotes, or articles), and some can be spontaneous (a comment on an industry story).

For an executive, your broadcast plan might have two arms. The first arm is that the executive's social media communication strategy must reflect the organization's values and the overall corporate plan. The overall corporate plan will typically reflect the 3-5 main messages or conversations the organization will be having externally. These conversations should reflect the organization's values and culture because the executives will also be setting the tone for employee communication as well as opening the door for partner communication.

The second arm of the executive social media plan is to identify your executive's personal platform, meaning the 2-3 primary things that he/she stands for. What are 2-3 things that are dear to his or her heart, whether business or personal, that can be shared with the world? How can he or she make this world a better place?

Let's look at Peter Aceto, CEO of ING Direct Canada. He has been using social media to engage consumers and build the ING Brand. This is what he has to say about tweeting his own personal agenda versus corporate branding:

I'm tweeting on behalf of our organization. It's me, it's not fake and I do all the writing myself and I share insights I have throughout the day—whether I'm in a meeting or I get an interesting leadership article. There's also some personal stuff in there because I have my own little agenda that isn't really an ING agenda, but it's about leaders, particularly CEOs and the stereotype that we have that I don't like very much. I'm trying to break down some barriers in terms of what it means to be a CEO.[10]

It's this personal touch, melded with the corporate touch that makes the executive human, makes you an individual and engages your team and the world.

The Fourth step in drafting your social media plan is to create "Buzz." Why do you want to create buzz? Because it means that you are successfully engaging people. You are drawing them in, entertaining them, educating them or informing them. They derive value from your association. Buzz is about touching people in a personal way. It's about building relationships.

When you are the organization, you totally want buzz because it increases your visibility, attracting more clients, partners and potential employees. But what if you are an executive or an individual contributor? How does buzz help you then?

As an executive buzz can increase employee engagement as they feel a stronger connection to you. It can attract more clients and reinforce the corporate brand. It can attract employees and partners. It can get you press.

Let's take a look again at Michael Rapino of LiveNation. If you look at his twitter feed, you will see that he successfully engages and responds to people. He forwards Instagram photos of concerts. He retweets industry blog articles and quotes. He tweets industry news and shares interviews of himself. He responds to comments. He talks to people. This is how you engage people and generate buzz or keep it going. It's about holding a conversation that anyone can listen to. All you have to do is ask questions and listen to others.

Once you have developed a relationship with your network, it's time to get them to "Buy." This is the fifth B of Social Media. When you are working on behalf of the organization, "buy" most often translates into "make a purchase." But in social media, "buy" simply means to "create a call to action." As an executive or spokesperson, that call-to-action can be anything—sign up for something, buy something, talk to me offline, write an article, tell me things I want to know, apply for a job with us, or any of a myriad of other options. As an employee, the call-to-action may simply be "respect me," "work with me" or "hire me."

One of the biggest mistakes most organizations make is that they focus all of their time and efforts on measuring sales or conversions. Social media success can be measured in many, many ways. What is most important is outlining your objectives clearly at the start and measuring against those objectives.

As you can see, executive and employee participation in social media can be an effective way to engage and grow your organization. A shift in cultural may be necessary, as determined by how closely your social media policy aligns with existing organizational values. Employee engagement can be aligned and guided to improve retention and facilitate growth through education and training. With proper planning and strategy, executive use of social media can also positively impact the bottom line. Links to additional resources available to assist in these efforts are noted in the appendix.

NOTES

1. IBM 2012 Global CEO Study, p. 35, Figure 10. http://public.dhe. ibm.com/common/ssi/ecm/en/gbe03485usen/GBE03485USEN. PDF

2. Consumers Engaged Via Social Media Are More Likely To Buy, Recommend, 2010, Chadwick Martin Bailey, http://blog.cmbinfo. com/press-center-content/bid/46920/Consumers-Engaged-Via-Social-Media-Are-More-Likely-To-Buy-Recommend

3. Consumers Engaged Via Social Media Are More Likely To Buy, Recommend, 2010, Chadwick Martin Bailey, http://blog.cmbinfo. com/press-center-content/bid/46920/Consumers-Engaged-Via-Social-Media-Are-More-Likely-To-Buy-Recommend

4. 2012 CEO.com Social CEO Report, p. 4., http://www.ceo.com/ wp-content/themes/ceo/assets/F500-Social-CEO-Index.pdf

5. 2012 CEO, Social Media & Leadership Survey, BrandFog, p. 20, http://www.brandfog.com/CEOSocialMediaSurvey/ BRANDfog_2012_CEO_Survey.pdf

6. IBM 2012 Global CEO Study, Figure 3.

7. The Social Divide - Employees, Executives Disagree on the Role of Social Media in Building Workplace Culture: Deloitte Survey http://www.deloitte.com/view/en_US/us/press/PressReleases/917e d0b3d26e7310VgnVCM2000001b56f00aRCRD.htm

8. 2012 CEO.com Social CEO Report, Infographic: How Social Are FORTUNE 500® CEOs? July 11, 2012. http://www.ceo.com/marketing/ infographic-how-social-are-fortune-500-ceos/#int=rtce303

9. 2012 CEO, Social Media & Leadership Survey, BrandFog, p. 12 http://www.brandfog.com/CEOSocialMediaSurvey/ BRANDfog_2012_CEO_Survey.pdf

10. Financial Post, "Executive tales from the Twitterverse: How ING Canada's CEO staked his brand on social media success", by Dan Ovsey | Jun 27, 2012 9:00 AM ET | Last Updated: Jun 27, 2012 3:38 PM ET. ", http://business.financialpost. com/2012/06/27/executive-tales-from-the-twitterverse-how-ing-canadas-ceo-staked-his-brand-on-social-media-success/

DAN BERRYMAN

About the Author

Dan Berryman is currently a VP of Investments with JP Morgan. He is a graduate of University of Oregon Business School. His passion and understanding of sales started with his first job as a sales representative with Procter & Gamble. At that time, Proctor & Gamble held the reputation for having the best consumer foods sales training program. Dan was part of their top producing national unit and later became Nestle's top performing northwest sales representative. Graduating first in his class in Shearson-Lehman Brothers' Investment Training, he later joined US Bank Investments. Dan became the top producing financial advisor and was promoted to District Sales Manager. He led his personal bankers to become the number one performing district in the Pacific North West. Since working with bank investment programs, he teaches, trains and coaches employees to master the fundamentals of the sales cycle and to increase their confidence: specifically, their ability to uncover and satisfy customer needs and overcome objections.

More information about Dan's Sales training resources is located on page 166.

Discover How to Sell Without "Selling"

By Helping People Get What They Want

by Dan Berryman

D oes the very mention of the word "Sell" or "Selling" make you sick? Are you automatically thinking to yourself right now, "I hate selling! Why am I even reading this chapter?" or "Thank God I'm not a sales person. That role is for someone who is comfortable being pushy!" Even if you're having those reactions, please keep reading, because what you're about to discover applies to everyone, every day, and that includes *You*!

It is a universal truth that *everyone* has painful experiences from the past—traumatic experiences arising from three main sources: Fear, rejection and danger. What's this have to do with selling? Let me explain.

Do you remember when you…

- Had an interview for a new job and were afraid that if asked a question you couldn't answer well, that you wouldn't be hired? How did you feel? Panic? Anxiety?
- How about when you asked someone out for a date and they said *NO*. How did you feel then? Rejection? Sick to your stomach?

• Or when you attended a family gathering where you're in the middle of a conversation and the topic switches to politics—and you just happen to be the only democrat among republicans—or visa versa. How were you feeling then? Fear of not fitting in? Maybe anger?

Believe it or not, each of these examples involved a *selling conversation*, and if you are like most people, the examples I just shared are infused with feelings of fear, rejection and danger. Consequently, doesn't the thought of having a selling conversation fill you with dread? Of course it does, because you don't want to come off as pushy, or you're secretly afraid of rejection or that you'll end up way out of your comfort zone, right? What if your co-workers, family or friends disagree with you? Will you then feel *outside* the circle of trust?

Imagine what would it be like if…

1. Instead of fear, rejection and anxiety, you actually get *excited* about having conversations with potential clients, family and friends and care about them so much you can *authentically connect* with them and help them get what they want—without ANY fear or hesitation of being too pushy?
2. How about when it comes to answering a question, or addressing a concern, you know exactly what to say, the perfect, clarifying questions to ask, and how to deal effectively with every response?
3. Lastly, from a business perspective, what if you know exactly what your clients/customers/staff/ boss/peers wanted and could consistently provide it to them?

This is what we will be discussing in more detail in this chapter. And just think, with the answers to these questions in hand, can you imagine how many more clients you would have, people you could help and money you would make?

Here is the absolute TRUTH: your ability to have genuine selling conversations is the key to having a thriving business, thriving relationships and a fulfilling life!

I'll share with you my five secrets in discovering *How to Sell Without Selling and Help People Get What They Want*, as well as the proven *4-Step Formula for Overcoming Objections*, which is designed specifically to reduce the stress, concerns and obstacles we encounter every day in our lives. Finally, you'll also learn how to run an *Objections Clinic*.

Before we dive into the secrets, let me you tell my story: Like so many others, I've struggled with my own personal demons around selling. My first job out of college was with Procter & Gamble. I didn't really want to be in sales; I felt that this was just an entry-level position to help me eventually go into *management* and climb the corporate ladder.

The company flew me back to Cincinnati for an intense one-week sales training program. On the first day, they informed us that we would be role-playing—on video—the Procter and Gamble *6 step selling presentation*. How did that make me feel? I had never done this before and I had always disliked hearing my voice on tape. That night, I experienced panic, fear, and *extreme* anxiety and had a sleepless night dreading the next day. What was happening to cause all these emotions? I was *way* outside of my comfort zone! My solution to this problem was, "I'll try it, and if it doesn't work out, I'll quit!" Fortunately, I made it through that week and when I got back home, my unit manager took me under his wing and we practiced, practiced and practiced.

What was the *main insight* he gave me? He said, "Dan, if you just learn to have an answer for every possible objection that could arise in a sales conversation, you'll be ok."

In review, what challenges did I face along the way? There was fear, rejection and the possibility of failure. My breakthrough came by understanding the process, having an answer for *every* objection, and then I practiced, practiced and practiced some more.

How did this whole experience transform me afterwards? I gained extreme confidence, started taking great pride in representing my company and its products and helped a lot of people along the way.

So let me ask you a question: Why should *you* listen to me and take the time to read about this subject? Because, having given over 37,000 sales presentations in my career (that's right, 37,000), I have had huge success. As a result, I have become a master at understanding how to ask the *right* questions, to discover what people *want* or *need*, and then I *give* it to them. It's that simple. I sell without "selling," by helping people get what they *want*.

Ever since graduating from the University of Oregon Business School, my entire professional career has been in sales. Over the past 20 years, I have been in the investment industry and am currently a Vice President and financial advisor with the nation's largest bank, JPMorgan Chase. I chose to work for their Investment Division because they currently have one of the top money management programs. I'm currently in the top 5% of Financial Advisors nationwide, managing money in this program. As a result of my success and experiences in the sales arena, I understand first-hand how important it is for you to have huge breakthroughs on this topic.

Secret #1: We are ALL in sales

This may come as a surprise to you. Are you ready? We all do it! We ALL do it. Do what? SELL! We all sell *every* day, in every human interaction that involves two or more people, where *opinions* are being *expressed*—we are selling. YOU are in sales. You might be thinking, "I *hate* those obnoxious and aggressive used car salesman types! I'm not *like* that and never will be." I agree whole-heartedly. However, what you have believed in the past about yourself and sales *might* not be true. I invite you to be open-minded and allow me to give you some *selling examples*.

Example #1: Upon arrival to this world as newborn babies, from the very first moment you wanted something from your mom or dad, you took some sort of action to get it. For most of us we "cried our heads off." That's right, you started the selling conversation as a baby and didn't even *know* it. However, what did you really want as a child? To be loved, accepted and safe. But all of us, to one degree or another, didn't *get* these needs met fully, so they became the *unconscious drive* behind most everything we did. This unconscious desire to be loved, accepted and safe fuels *most* decisions we make to this day.

Example #2: As a teenager, remember how strongly you felt about something, or you had an opinion that just made *no* sense to mom and dad? You had to use the *same* skills that are used in business every day to prove your point and *influence the outcome.* In other words, make the sale! And if your idea was rejected, remember how upset you became and how you felt?

Example #3: You're at a party and you see an attractive woman and you start forming your "sales presentation" of why she would want to go out with you. Your "sales pitch" has probably gotten a lot better cause you've had *lots* of practice.

All these examples were about us making *selling* presentations to get something. So if we *all* do it and we do it all the time, why don't we like to do it? Like I said, because sometimes we get shut down—Failure! Rejection! Pain!

Secret #2: We hate sales because it brings up our fears

Remember my example about asking someone on a date and you got shut down? These painful, traumatic experiences arose from three main sources:

- FEAR—or in other words, not feeling loved.
- REJECTION—or in other words, not feeling accepted, prompting competition and comparison.
- DANGER—or in other words, not feeling safe.

Do you see where I'm going with this? Let's see how our negative experiences in trying to *meet* these unconscious needs have influenced our *dislike* for sales. To restate the problem: Why do we hate selling? Because we have been traumatized by these experiences. Remember our basic needs are to be loved, accepted and safe? But because most of us weren't so fortunate to have these needs met *consistently*, we ended up in adulthood with feelings and memories of *fear* and *rejection*; just the *opposite* emotions of *love, acceptance* and *safety*.

The reason why *businesses* struggle with selling conversations is because their employees hate selling too! For a lot of us, selling feels pushy. It feels strange and awkward, or it sometimes seems without integrity. And it's been *my* experience that the *majority* of individuals I've managed, coached and trained *focus* on the word SELL. When they do this, they either consciously or subconsciously react with *their own* memories of fear, rejection and feeling unsafe. So unless we do healing work around this fear, rejection and danger, we'll *continue* to have an aversion to selling. What is our *solution* to all this pain around selling?

Secret #3: *Change your state of mind* around selling

I invite you to shift your thinking about the *selling conversation* and experience a breakthrough. When you're in sales, and when it's done consciously, you're providing a *service* to people, where clients really do *benefit*. And *that*, my friend, is a noble thing. Our goal in sales is *not* to try and *convince* anyone that they want what *you* are selling, using *force* and *coercion* by telling them what to do. The goal is to help people remove any obstacles to attract what they already know they want.

And why is it so *crucial* that we learn how to have empowered selling conversations? Because in business, no matter what your position, this is where your income comes from. So we need to be *really clear* on that. Your income doesn't come from marketing or advertising or any other source, even if these do draw customers to your company. Everyone's paycheck comes directly or indirectly from *conscious* sales people sitting down and having a genuine, connecting conversation, where we find out what someone wants or needs, see if our product or service is a fit, and if so, we make an invitation to them to work with us.

By understanding that selling is a *normal* part of everyday interactions between people, and if we are *all* involved in sales conversations every day, you can then relax and embrace sales as a natural, healthy, normal conversation, and your potential clients will take your lead and relax into your conversation as well, because you are genuinely interested in *meeting their needs*.

Secret #4: People don't do things to you, they do things for themselves

So if people do things for themselves, what is it exactly they want? Remember? They want to be loved, accepted and safe. Let's reiterate: People don't do things to you, like *intentionally* reject you, but they do things for themselves. This means it's all about them! Doesn't that take the pressure off, now that you know it's not about *you*? Now, you can relax and master the answers to their main objections and share your product's features and benefits. When what you have to offer is the right fit for them, you become an expert at empowering them to make a decision right now…they're just waiting for you to ask!

Secret #5: People do things for one of two reasons—to gain a benefit or avoid a loss

The *benefit* they seek is around the issue of love and acceptance. Avoiding a *loss* is around the issue of safety. So yes, once again it's all about them and not about you! Why? Because everything we do is motivated by the drive for love, acceptance and safety. As I just mentioned, when we get something we want, this is tied to feeling loved and accepted. When we try to avoid something we don't want, this is tied to danger or not feeling safe. Sounds simple, right? But I didn't say it was easy...

If we can just figure out how to help people gain a benefit or avoid a loss, and if what you offer is a fit for them, then you're on your way to a genuine sale! And if we keep this knowledge in our consciousness, then we don't have to take it personally when someone says, "NO." It's not about you! Does that help?

I hope by now you are ready for me to invite you to adopt *my* definition of selling, which is this: Empowering people to make a decision that helps them get what they want.

Now that we are starting to see sales in a whole new light, let's explore the *4-step formula for Overcoming Objections* and massively increase your confidence level before, during and after the selling conversation.

I have found that out of the entire sales cycle, the ability to handle objections and overcome obstacles will increase a person's confidence faster than anything else. No one on earth likes it when someone says "NO" to them and you don't know what to say. These are known as objections. They are the "yeah, buts" that block a sale. You need to know what to do when someone says, "Yeah, but I'm not interested," or, "Yeah, but that's too expensive," or, "Yeah, but let me think about it."

If we anticipate the objections ahead of time and have a system like my 4-step formula, you can set things up in advance so that you are prepared for those objections. If you've thought about them ahead of time, and you have a plan for how you're going to handle them, you are going to feel so confident in dealing with them that you'll be telling yourself, "I *know* what objections might come up and if they do, here's how I'll help myself and my clients get through them."

While in management, one of my personal bankers—a woman who had recently immigrated to the US—told me, "Dan, I'll never forget the training you gave where you told us that when we sat down with a potential client to discuss products and services, we would hear only 8-10 common objections and to write them all down and come up with an effective response for each concern so that regardless of whether they make a purchase, there is nothing they can say or ask you don't *already* have an answer to." She went on to become one of the top performing personal bankers in Oregon.

Here is the 4-step formula I want you to follow:

1) Restate (or clarify the concern)
2) Validate (empathize to show understanding)
3) Respond (explain or inform)
4) Confirm (test for acceptance)

I'll share a personal example of how the 4-step process works in my day-to-day job. As a Financial Advisor for JPMorgan Chase, over the past three years, clients have been referred to me who have purchased Certificates of Deposit. They were very popular for our clients because at the time they were paying 4-5% interest and the principle was FDIC insured. When these CDs mature, the money needs to be reinvested, but in today's market CDs are only paying 1-2%, and that low rate does *not* interest them. When a CD client comes to see me, the first thing they say is, "I'm not interested in any investments unless they are FDIC insured and I want a higher rate than 2%." So let's use *this objection* in our 4-step process:

Step1—Restate (clarify the concern)

"Ms. Client, if I understand you correctly, you are not interested in any investment that is not FDIC insured?"
  • Restating keeps the conversation going. Just because someone expresses a concern, it doesn't mean the conversation is over.

- Restating lets the prospect know you are listening and really *hearing* their concern

Step 2—Validate (empathize to show understanding)

"You know, Ms. Client, I understand how you feel. Several clients of mine, just like yourself, have had CDs mature and *also* wanted only FDIC insured investments."

There are three components here:

- Acknowledging—It doesn't mean you agree, but when you acknowledge, you respond in a way that shows you have *understood* them.
- Paraphrasing—involves summarizing what the prospect said.
- Empathizing—adds the important dimension concerning how the client *feels* about what has been said.

Remember that good listening skills show you hear, care and understand. For example: Ms. Client, I *understand* that you are concerned about safety. Most of my clients *feel* the same way… Ms. Client, I *understand* that you are *concerned* about the cost… Ms Client, I can *understand* how you might *feel* this way…"

Step #3—Respond (explain how your idea works with the appropriate facts, features and benefits)

"Ms. Client, here's what they found: First of all, most people like CDs because they are low risk. We have a government bond fund that is *also* considered low risk and the US Government backs *every* bond in the portfolio. As a result, your principle and interest on the bonds are *guaranteed*. What this means to you is that you don't lose sleep at night. Secondly, last year my clients earned 5.5%, and year-to-date we are up 4%. What this means to you is *more money in your pocket*. Tell me, Ms. Client, would you be *interested* in earning 4–5% with safety?" In step #3 is where you address four specific components with the client:

1. You provide Facts—what is true and not subjective.
2. You state the Features—defined as the characteristics of a product or service. Your client will only buy when they can clearly understand how the *features* will *benefit* them.
3. Interject the Transition Statement—which connects the feature to the benefit in the client's mind. *"What this means to you..."*
4. You state the Benefits—defined as something a product or service will *do for* the client and answers their primary concern: *"What's in it for me?"*

Here's an example of step #3 coming together: I'll first state the feature, then the transition phrase and finally the benefit. Feature: Mr. Client, JP Morgan Chase has one of the highest all-American rated research teams in the country. Transition: What this means to you is… Benefit: we have the ability to put you in touch with some of the best investment advice available anywhere.

Step #4—Confirm (check back in with the client)

"Ms. Client, before we discuss this investment in more detail, does this address your concern about looking at low risk investments?"

Here is where you need to *test for acceptance*. If appropriate, continue questioning and exploring other *need* areas.

In review, *every* objection that arises can be answered with this four-step process: Restate, validate, respond and confirm. Once these steps are *mastered* and become second nature, your confidence level will *skyrocket*. And how do you create a standard process for teaching the objections unique to your company's product or service? Let me leave you with something that will help. It's called an Objections Clinic. You can have an Objections Clinic specialist come in and administer this clinic or do it yourself. What is *The Objections Clinic*? This is where you have a group meeting to do the following:

- You gather all the objections surrounding your product or service. And by the way, employees *love* this process because they can't *wait* to tell you *all* the objections they hear and why *they can't sell.*
- Then you gather all the answers by breaking into groups for script writing—using the *4-step formula for overcoming objections.* After answers have been developed and tested on prospects in real selling conversations, then you do a *post-clinic follow-up* to ask the following questions:
- Are there any objections that surfaced that we didn't anticipate? If yes, do an emergency Objections Clinic.
- Are the answers working? If no, do an emergency Objections Clinic and *brainstorm* different answers.
- What are the most *frequent* objections you are hearing? Typically 20% of the objections are doing 80% of the damage. This last question helps determine which objections are the most common so that employees will be especially prepared to deal with them.

The Objections Clinic—by itself—has been responsible for doubling and tripling sales, so I strongly encourage you to implement this as a normal practice…ASAP.

Now that we've uncovered why we all do it (selling), and now that we understand what's really happening in a sales conversation; that in spite of our fears that come up it *isn't* about us, *and* you've changed your state of mind about having sales conversations, and I've given you a taste of my 4-step proven formula for handling objections, what's next? Now, the only thing that's left to do is *practice.* In summary:

- Understand that when people say "no" to you, they aren't rejecting you. You just haven't been able to help them avoid a loss or gain the benefit they were seeking.
- When you change your state of mind and see selling as nothing more than meeting needs, then sales becomes a noble function because you are being of *service.*
- When you have ready answers to the most common objections, then your sales closing ratio will steadily increase, and when some-

one does says "no," even after executing the 4-step process, you'll understand what's going on, not take it personally and move on to the next person you can help.

• When you empower the client to make the decision to purchase from you, it's a *triple* win!

1) The client prospers because you have met a need and they get what they want.
2) You prosper because you have the satisfaction of being of service and you earned a profit.
3) Your company prospers from the sale.

One last thing about sales: I'm going to give you permission to fail. Am I crazy? Nobody wants to fail! But think about it: The people we admire the most, we admire because they tried and failed several times until they became masters of their game. Have you heard the saying, "Imperfect action is always better than perfect inaction?" It's true. So if you give yourself permission to fail, and see each failure as a learning experience to hone your skills and become better at identifying and meeting needs, then you will be able to jump in and try what we're talking about, knowing that any practice you do will lead to more success.

And when you're in that selling conversation and fear comes up, take some deep breaths and become conscious of what is really going on and *remind* yourself that *conscious* selling is nothing more than helping people get what they want, and THAT is noble. When you focus on this thought, it doesn't take much to shift the energy from fear into excitement!

I invite you to remember, we all do it—sell—so isn't it time we face our fears and figure out how to do it *well*, which means learning how to empower people to make a decision that meets their needs? Now go out and *sell without selling* by giving people what they *want*…and prosper!

JUDITH HURLBURT, M.ED.

About the Author

Judith Hurlburt, NLP Trainer's Trainer, is a dynamic, engaging, longtime educator of children and adults. She has worked in schools, in small and large businesses, in government and non-profit agencies, in her own business, and in one-to-one relationships. She excels at curriculum and training design at all levels. Judith has created and directed multimillion-dollar systemic change projects, has developed cutting edge curriculum for adults and children, and planned and led a wide variety of staff development trainings. Judith is a successful project consultant and evaluator, grantwriter and grant writing trainer. She is known for her creativity, integrity, passion for learning, and capacity to see issues from different perspectives and create and deliver new possibilities. Judith is committed to supporting individuals and companies through life's surprises, perceived losses, and desired changes, helping them discover possibilities within and without, and throughout their lives. Judith is dedicated to helping others in learning, exploring possibilities, manifesting outcomes, and developing *strategies for long-lasting change—the unexpected...and the desired.*

More information about Judy is available on page 168.

The Power of Purpose as *Life Happens*

by Judith Hurlburt

Y‌ou've seen the wall hanging or bumper sticker that says, "The worst day fishing beats the best day at work!" Substitute any word or phrase for fishing and you have an attitude many people hold toward their work. Fishing and work have different purposes. The main purpose for fishing is "relaxation and getting away from it all," while one of the main purposes for working is financial stability. When people dig deeper into their purpose for working, they are likely to find more purposes than financial stability. Most who dig deeper are likely to find that the purposes of work are something like the following:

- To feel useful.
- To feel a sense of worth beyond money.
- To feel motivated by the results of work.
- To have a place that feeds interests and fascinations.
- To feel recognized for contributions by the company.
- To work and socialize with people around common interests, ideas and values.

- To structure time, experiences, talents and skills.
- To be a good model for children (grandchildren, friends).
- To share talents and to do good for others.
- To achieve status in one's field of expertise.

Purpose is what gets us up in the morning and gets us off to work. Purpose is the reason and the motivation for going to work. The purpose for work goes beyond the company's leave policies, and negotiated agreements and contracts. Those policies and agreements, as well as vision and mission statements, all support the overall purpose of the company. Business leaders will likely discover that, like an individual, the purposes upon which the company was built go beyond finances. In addition to profit, the company's purposes might sound something like these:

- To build and support a community of workers that brings stability to our town.
- To provide financial stability to the entire region.
- To create jobs for students leaving college and wanting to return to the community.
- To share our profit with those needing shoes.
- To help people heal after accidents.
- To provide dental services to the underserved in the surrounding communities.
- To support the development of creative minds that produce profitable products.
- To provide project management that completes projects within stated timeframes.

If company and personal purposes align, work can be as motivating and engaging as fishing or other leisure-time activities. People work because they have purposes beyond financial stability. Many work because they love and are motivated by it what they do. Most have lives outside work, even though work fills many of their waking hours.

As another bumper sticker says, "Sh** Happens" (*Life Happens*). *Life*

Happens in the form of desired changes. *Life Happens* in the form of unexpected changes. When *Life Happens* to a business leader individually, or to employees, the company is impacted because personal and work lives are part of the same fabric. The purpose of this chapter is to share four common scenarios to stretch your thinking beyond the vision, mission, goals, policies and negotiated agreements and to have you consider the power of purpose. Each scenario provides at least one strategy for using your company's purposes to engage and retain employees as *Life Happens* to them. The last two scenarios include strategies for how to capitalize on an employee's purposes for work to help your company grow as *Life Happens*.

Scenario #1

You are deep into a project. The objectives have so far been successfully met within the allotted timeframes. Projected costs and revenues are on target, and it appears the project will complete successfully within six weeks. It is with a sense of excitement that you go into work earlier than usual to have a few quiet minutes to review an upcoming project. You see a light in the office of Ellen, an employee critical to the successful project. Initially you assume she, too, simply wanted a few minutes of uninterrupted time before the rush of the day. But, as you walk by her door to get coffee you see she has her head down on folded arms on her desktop. You pause and decide to investigate because this is so uncharacteristic of Ellen. You enter her office, knock gently on the partially closed door, and quietly say her name. She jerks awake in confusion and lets her head fall back into her arms. She takes a deep breath, pauses, and then says, "What am I going to do? What are WE going to do? I received a phone call late last night from my husband's best friend. They were on a fishing trip and were in a terrible car accident. Tom is in the hospital in a coma with multiple injuries and has been heavily sedated. I have spoken with the doctor and have made the earliest reservation I could. I leave this morning at 8 o'clock. My best friend is staying with the kids. I came into work to get as much done as I could before I left to be with him. I feel so awful leaving right now, but I have to go. What will you do?"

What *will* you do? Clearly Ellen has gotten out of bed many mornings and has been instrumental in the project's success. She's had some underlying purpose other than the project's goals and objectives and timelines. She is experiencing one of those *Life Happens* events over which neither of you have control. What you do have control over is how you respond both in the short term and the long term to Ellen.

A healthy, collaborative company culture will have as one of its purposes something like: "To build and support a community of workers that bring stability to our town." You might have another purpose about completing projects within timeframes. Now is the time to call up those purposes. You can impact the long-range outcome of this event on the company as well as on Ellen.

According to research, any loss creates a change in the chemistry of the body. In order to help stabilize her body chemistry, Ellen needs support. At the same time you want to support her, you want to find ways for the project to move forward within timeframes without Ellen. In order to accomplish both, focus on the underlying purpose of supporting Ellen.

Strategy #1-1: To use purpose to provide initial support and engage an employee.

1. Simply ask, "What happened?"
2. JUST LISTEN with no comments or suggestions.

At times of loss, listening is the most critical thing you can do. At this moment, Ellen isn't thinking clearly about the project. If you listen she can release some of the shock to her system and may be able to engage for a few minutes on a short-term plan. Her capacity to engage is compromised and likely will be for a period of time. Her immediate purpose is to help her husband survive and recover while at the same time caring for her children. The company's project is further down the list of her priorities at this moment.

Ellen knows she is critical to the project. The success of the project is likely critical to her feeling of well-being. When supported, the same purposes for which Ellen had engaged in the project in the first place will have a chance to resurface—AFTER her other purposes have been mostly fulfilled.

3. After Ellen describes what happened, tell her you are sorry for her loss. Yes, it is a loss. Her husband's incapacity is a form of loss. Assure her someone will contact the Human Relations Department to get her leave and insurance issues addressed.

4. In the few minutes Ellen may be able to engage with any coherence, ask her a few specific questions. Specific questions will focus her attention and allow her to engage for a short period of time. They draw upon what can come easily to her because she's so familiar with the project. Ask:

   • Who are you working with at this time? Who knows the project best?

   • What is one next action that needs to happen? One!

   • By when do you want that action completed?

   • Where is your documentation on the project? Where specifically is documentation on the one next step?

   • How specifically would you organize resources to complete that next step?

5. Now, let her go to focus on other priorities. Ask her what kind of support she needs, like anything from a ride to the airport to someone to help her find files. Assure her the project will continue to move forward with the information she's given you. Let her know she is welcome to call anytime,

and that at least for a few days you want her to focus on her husband. Assume that small steps can be made toward project completion. Be honest with Ellen's coworkers, and be honest with project stakeholders. Strategies for those types of conversations can be addressed in another training.

Now fast forward several days when Ellen is back at work. Her husband is still in the hospital and will have to go to rehab at a live-in facility in another week. The purposes she had for engaging in the project are beginning to resurface, though she is still numb and her capacity to think clearly remains compromised. When you ask her how things are going she says she's worried because there are many items to address in order for the project to complete on time. Your purpose now is to support her engagement so the project can continue toward on-time completion.

Strategy #1-2: To use purpose to provide ongoing support and engage an employee.

1. Ask Ellen to quickly list what needs to be completed within 5 days.
2. Then ask, "What is ONE action you can complete **today** that will move the project forward and fulfill the purpose of completing the project on time? Just ONE action." When Ellen responds, let her know you'll check in with her to see what progress she's made toward the one action. Assure her that even one action will serve the purpose of moving the project forward. By asking Ellen to focus her attention on one item, her energy begins moving. Her energy will no longer be focused on the overwhelming long list of items. Once she's engaged with the one action, she *might* be able to keep moving forward on more than one action. When you check in with her later, only inquire

about the one action. Let both of you be surprised if she has accomplished more than one item on her list.

Ellen's original purpose for getting up and coming to work can be fulfilled in small steps—one at a time. Fulfilling her purposes in a step-by-step fashion will help keep Ellen stabilized as her husband recovers.

3. Allow time for Ellen to re-engage fully in her work as she fulfills other higher priority purposes in her life after the loss.

Scenario #2

Eric walks into your office and asks if he can talk with you. You agree, and he closes the door, his face drawn and tight. He drops into the chair and announces, "I am turning in my resignation to be effective as soon as possible." You're somewhat taken aback because Eric has been a very good employee, and appears to have liked working for the company.

Strategy #2-1: To explore purposes to retain an employee.

1. Ask, "What happened that got you to this point of resigning?"
2. JUST LISTEN with no comments or suggestions.

As Eric begins talking you remember he applied for a promotion into another position. He didn't get the promotion. You suspected he'd felt disappointed when he was turned down, but he had not spoken with you about it. To you, he had appeared to go on with his work without being impacted by his disappointment. Eric had come to the conclusion that he wasn't valued by the company. He thought that his work really didn't matter other than the profit it brought the company. He felt disappointed that he wasn't valued. After thinking for several weeks about not getting the new position, Eric decided he wanted to resign and began to look for work elsewhere. It appears Eric has lost his reasons for getting out of bed in the morning and coming to work. His purposes for work might have changed due to his disappointment. Because you want to retain Eric in the company and in your department if possible, now is a good time to focus the conversation on Eric's purposes for working for the company.

3. Ask the following questions and follow each one with, "What else?" After three responses, simply repeat Eric's responses. (This strategy is taken from the work of Christina Hall, Ph.D., and owner of The NLP Connection.)
   • What motivated you to seek that new position? What else? What else?
   So you were motivated to apply by x, y and z.
   • What was interesting to you about that position? What else? What else?
   So you were interested in that position because of x, y and z.
   • What else about that position drew you to it? Anything else?
4. Repeat again all the things Eric said were motivating and interesting and drew him to the new position, and then ask, "For what overall purpose did you want the new position?"
5. Then say, "So the purposes for seeking the new position were to earn a larger salary, to have new challenges and learn new things, meet new people, and get re-motivated about coming to work."
6. Assure Eric that he is valued by you, he's done excellent work in this department, and you've counted on him to provide creative thinking and new ideas.
7. Based on his purposes for applying for the new position, ask if he's willing to explore possibilities in this department that might meet some of those purposes as well. Using his responses, you ask what the salary was for the new position, how his current position might be reorganized so he could learn new things and

have new challenges. Explore together how he might stay in this position and be able to meet new people. Ask what it would take to re-motivate him to stay in this department with new challenges.

8. After the discussion, ask Eric,
   - "How willing are you to reconsider your decision to resign by focusing on the questions I've posed to you?"
   - "How willing are you to have me explore possibilities for changing some aspects of your position so you could become re-motivated to stay."
   - "How much time do you need to reconsider?"
   - "When can we meet again to discuss the new possibilities?"

You helped Eric explore and define his new purposes for his work. While you are exploring possibilities for changing his position, revisit your company's purposes. See if you can find one such as "to support the development of creative minds that produce profitable products." Determine if the company's purposes match Eric's new purposes for work. Share those purposes when you meet again with Eric and work together to realign his purposes with the company's purposes.

Focusing on an employee's purposes for coming to work can be a powerful conversation that can help retain a valued employee. It is easy to get derailed by immediate losses and changes and lose focus on the overall purposes for being at work. The strategies above can be applied to many scenarios in which *Life Happens* and an employee wants to resign or move to another position. Other examples that could use these strategies for resigning are a divorce from a spouse that either works for the company or a closely related company, the seeming inability to re-engage after the loss of a loved one and the belief that quitting is better than struggling to come to work, or an unexpected pregnancy for a woman who loves her work yet knows her priorities will shift with the birth of the baby.

The previous two scenarios explored how purpose can be used to engage and retain an employee when *Life Happens.* Scenarios 3 and 4 demonstrate how to capitalize on unexpected events to grow and expand your company. Feel how focusing on purposes in the next two scenarios can change an employee's sense of purpose and allow you to expand.

Scenario #3

Susan appears in your office one morning several days after the funeral for her husband, Alex. She's been a valued employee and her colleagues have missed her while she's been on leave after the death. Alex's sudden, unexpected death impacted Susan's colleagues and management because Alex was young and many people knew him quite well from social occasions. In addition, colleagues thought highly of Alex because he was very supportive of Susan's career. Susan closes the door and asks to talk with you because she has decided to move.

Strategy #3-1: To capitalize on unexpected events and expand your company.

1. Ask, "What happened to get you to this point of moving?"
2. JUST LISTEN with no comments or suggestions.

Susan goes on, "After much consideration I've decided to move across the state so I have the support of both my husband's and my extended families. We have friends here, but if you remember, Alex and I took the kids to see their grandparents, aunts, uncles and cousins at least once a month. We wanted them to know their extended family and feel their love and support. With Alex gone now, I'll be totally responsible for the kids alone. I don't think I can do a good job on my own. I've talked with my family and with Alex's family, and they would love to have us closer. So…I'm moving and will have to resign from my job here."

You've just been handed a possibility of a way to expand the company's market with a trusted employee to whom one of those unexpected events happened. Focus on the company's purpose of supporting employees and building community, as well as on the company's newly established long-term goal of expanding its market across the state.

3. Clarify with Susan that her purpose for leaving the company is to move closer to support for herself and her children.
4. Explore her purposes for working in the company for the past several years.
5. If her reason for leaving the company is to be near her family, ask her this question:, "How possible is it you would consider taking the lead and helping establish a branch of the company in a town on the other side of the state, near your families?"

You support Susan as *Life Happens*, capitalize on the opportunity to help her maintain some stability in her life by being able to fulfill her purposes for work, and at the same time possibly meet a long-term goal that supports the company's purposes.

Scenario #4

The department's social committee has arranged a luncheon for Roxanne, a beloved high level administrative assistant who is getting married. She's worked in the company for several years, and for you for four of them. You think highly of her, and you attend. Life is happening to her in a desired, positive way. During the luncheon you overhear Roxanne describing her future husband, Rick, and worrying he is moving to town just before the wedding, but hasn't found work yet. He's excited about getting married but a little concerned about finding work using computer skills and his new IT degree.

Strategy #4-1: To capitalize on a desired event and expand your company.

1. At an appropriate moment, engage Roxanne in a conversation about Rick's skills. Ask what his goal is for using his computer skills and IT degree. You learn that Rick's long-term goal is to start his own company and contract with companies. Ask what Rick's purpose is for starting his own company rather than seeking employment with a company such as yours. You learn that the main purpose for establishing his own company is so Rick can work from home and be the main support parent when the couple has children.

2. Ask Roxanne to have Rick schedule an appointment with you to discuss the possibility of a contract with the company. Again, you realize you might be able to fulfill several company purposes and needs as *Life Happens* to Roxanne. You focused on the company's purpose to build and support a community of workers, to provide jobs for college graduates, and the company's need for more IT support. You may be able to meet some of your need for more IT support without hiring a full-time, benefited employee. In addition you will be supporting Rick's purposes for establishing his own company, and you will be able to retain Roxanne's valuable skills and experience for several years into the future.

In conclusion, *"Life Happens,"* just as the bumper sticker says, "SH** Happens." Desired and unexpected changes happen every day. The components of the scenarios presented can be interchanged with a variety of different events. Death, divorce, illness, change in family status, moves, and changes at work all constitute *Life Happens.* In order to lessen the impact when *Life Happens*, focus on the purposes of the company, and on the purposes that draw your employees to work each day. Think beyond the vision, goals, mission statement, policies and procedures. Think "above all," to overriding purposes of what makes the employee get out of bed in the morning and come to work instead of "going fishing." Focusing on overall purposes helps stabilize employees and lessens the impact on them and the company when they experience changes. Act purposefully as *Life Happens*, by utilizing the simple strategies of:

- Listening without comment except to say, "I'm sorry," as someone talks about the loss,
- Asking only a few specific questions to engage someone whose capacity to engage is compromised,
- Focusing on completing one action at a time toward project goals when an employee is finding it hard to engage in work,
- Allowing time for an employee to re-engage fully once they fulfill other higher priority purposes,
- Asking specific questions and exploring a resigning employee's purposes for working at the company,
- Capitalizing on possibilities for expansion and growth as *Life Happens* to you and employees.

Explore and utilize both the company's purposes and employees' purposes to make the "best day at work" as good or better than fishing.

Copyright © 2012 Judith Hurlburt

IDA SHESSEL, B.Sc., M.Ed.

About the Author

Ida Shessel, B.Sc., M.Ed. is a leading expert in engaging, encouraging, and empowering others. She is the CEO of Ida Shessel International, Inc.

For the past 30 years, she has been helping leaders and their team members become dynamic communicators and overcome typical communication challenges. She has delivered thousands of motivational and competency-based programs at conferences, colleges, and meetings across North America and beyond.

Ida has worked with the U.S. Department of Homeland Security, The Hartford Financial Services Group, Canadian Broadcasting Corporation, Microsoft Corporation, GlaxoSmithKline, State University of New York, and many more organizations. She is the author of Communicate Like a Top Leader and Meeting with Success.

More information about Ida Shessel International, Inc. is available on page 170.

Your Best Meeting Ever

Leading Meetings that Engage,
Encourage and Empower Others

by Ida Shessel

"No one ever participates at meetings." This is a common complaint voiced frequently across many types of organizations. Why don't employees participate at meetings? The problem is not the meeting itself. After all, most people enjoy being with other people. Rather, it's *how* they meet. The meeting leader puts out the coffee and the muffins...and hopes that something good will happen.

Meetings are costly time wasters. American economist John Kenneth Galbraith once said, "Meetings are indispensable when you don't want to do anything." The ugly truth is that meetings have deteriorated to the point of being unfocused and unproductive. They zap employee energy and productivity as well as organizational time and money.

Meetings that lack participation from attendees waste the talent, skills, experience, knowledge and creativity sitting in the room. There is synergy that can be harnessed to grow the organization as well as the individuals within it by solving problems, making decisions, developing new products and services, improving processes and procedures, and teaching others.

A meeting brings together a diverse group of individuals with differing personalities, expectations, cultures, goals, issues and working styles that needs to be collaborating successfully for the good of the organization. As a result, there are bound to be challenges.

In this chapter you'll learn ten strategies you can implement to overcome some of your meeting challenges, ramp up participation from attendees and tap into the value that others bring to your meetings. As an added bonus, you'll find key principles and strategies that can be applied not *just* to a meeting environment but to any area of business or life.

Strategy 1: Shift Your "Participation" Paradigm

What exactly is participation? At a meeting with an accounting firm, the managing partner remarked in a frustrated tone of voice, "Our employees don't participate in meetings."

"Participate," according to Webster's dictionary, is defined as "to take part, be or become actively involved, or share (in)." It seems obvious, but bear with me here for a minute.

Every time a client says to me, "My staff won't participate or speak up in meetings," I hear a built-in assumption that the only way for people to participate in a meeting is for each of them to verbally address the entire group.

Please consider this: The participation does not have to be verbal, nor does it have to be directed to the entire group. If you are looking for input from attendees in the form of opinions, analysis, suggestions and more, there are various ways of achieving that goal. If you look at the definition again, you will not find any restrictions or guidelines on *how* participation is supposed to happen, so expand your thinking!

Let us agree that it does not matter *how* your staff members participate, only that they do. From now on, consider participation as consisting of any combination of the following four elements:

- There is a task (discussion, idea generation, update, problem-solving, decision-making, evaluation).
- Any combination of people can work on the task (the entire group together, individuals or small groups).
- The results of the task can be submitted in either written or oral form.
- The task can take any length of time.

For example, an individual can participate by spending one minute thinking about and then generating one idea and submitting it to you orally. In another situation, you might have a group of four employees engaging in problem-solving for fifteen minutes and recording a list of possible solutions on an easel chart or a presentation slide. Alternatively, a group of two spends half an hour brainstorming several times over the course of a week. You get the idea.

With this broader perspective of what participation means, you have many more options for how people can participate in your meetings. Further on in the chapter you will learn about orchestrating participation.

Strategy 2: Clarify the Type of Meeting You are Leading

There are various types of get-togethers that all seem to fall under the category of "meetings." Goals, expectations and results will differ from one meeting type to another. The following are common types of meetings by purpose:

- Presentation with the intent of making others aware of something ("one-way" delivery only).
- Town hall meeting with the entire department or organization (with a dedicated Q&A period).
- Smaller (weekly) meeting with direct reports, in which there are issues, problems, strategies, goals, or decisions up for discussion.
- Training session, where those present are expected to either acquire new or enhance existing skills, behaviors, or attitudes.

• Celebration of an accomplishment, merger, or annual financial results.

• Special-event retreat where creative problem-solving or mission and vision development need to take place.

Once you clarify the type of meeting you are going to have, you'll be better equipped to invite the right attendees, craft the right objectives, plan the right activities and assign the right tasks. Hiring a neutral outside facilitator might even be a good thing to do.

Strategy 3: Consider the Causes

Some attendees are not comfortable speaking up in a large group. It doesn't matter how many times you say to the group "I want your input," it still won't happen. There are many possible reasons. Some of the attendees…

• Are afraid of appearing stupid.

• Don't have the self-confidence to speak up in a large group.

• Don't believe that their input is truly valued.

• Feel intimidated by aggressive, bullying behavior or snide remarks of others.

• Are afraid that their ideas will be shot down.

• Want to wait and see how other attendees' ideas are received.

• Need inspiration, thinking time or research time because they really do lack ideas.

• Need time to warm up.

• Don't want to repeat ideas already mentioned by the group's more vocal members.

• Feel they are "off the hook" when others are doing the talking (and the work).

• Aren't motivated by or interested in the topic.

• Are distracted by other things at work or home.

- Feel intimidated by the status of some of the dominant participants in the room.
- Feel that their language skills are not good enough to make their ideas clear to the others.
- Have grown up in a culture that forbids or discourages voicing opinions in front of, contradicting or asking questions of an authority figure or an elder.

Note the last bullet point. A financial institution that I have worked with experiences this challenge on a daily basis. A large percentage of the staff is Asian. Even though the leaders want their employees to adjust to the North American style of interacting with those higher up in the organization and they have emphasized that they want employee participation, it may take years for the staff to adjust, if they ever do.

Is it possible that some of these causes are holding your attendees back from full participation?

Strategy 4: Orchestrate Participant Involvement

As you learned earlier, the definition of participation makes no mention of the manner in which someone takes part in a meeting. That leaves it open to many possibilities.

Consider using group work. In my 30+ years of leading interactive workshops and meetings, I have engineered participation through group work many times. It's foolproof! When it is done properly (and we will get to that), assigned group work rarely fails to encourage attendees to participate. Imagine having an entire room full of people participating simultaneously—generating ideas, discussing the pros and cons of various alternatives and building solutions.

This method works because many people are more comfortable and productive working on a task on their own or with only two or three other people. Why fight it? Why insist on only one method of participation—

large group discussion? By using a variety of methods, you address differing learning styles and working styles. You will also increase the likelihood that the quieter attendees contribute—and one of them may have that million-dollar idea!

Group work also serves as an antidote to many of the issues listed above in *Consider the Causes*. When assigned a task in small groups, attendees often feel more accountable for results and work toward fulfilling that responsibility. Many of the issues holding them back in the large group environment are diminished in a smaller, more intimate group setting.

Note that the size of the group matters enormously. A group of, say, 8 will often produce close to the same number and types of anxieties as a group of 20. Groups of 3 or 4 mean exactly that—groups of 3 or 4, no matter how administratively awkward this size may be.

It is important to maintain confidentiality or anonymity. There may be situations in which your employees would be willing to provide input as long as they are not identified as the source of the information or comment. Ease some of their anxieties by using input-gathering techniques that protect participant identities.

There are also times when meetings need to be short and sweet. If there isn't going to be time for brainstorming activities during the meeting, let the participants know well ahead of time what you expect from them. By sending out the agenda, the objectives and the assignments one week in advance (or more, depending on the topic and the situation), you are giving them thinking time. They can conduct whatever research is necessary and then come to the meeting brimming with ideas. Springing an issue or question on them without any forewarning is a recipe for failure. For some people, their best ideas come as afterthoughts. If you want creative, realistic, and well-thought-out input, set participants up for success.

Share the roles and responsibilities. Ask for volunteers to take on such roles as facilitator, topic leader or presenter, timekeeper and note taker.

When others share in the responsibilities of the meeting, they automatically become more engaged and empowered. They also have opportunities to grow, honing valuable skills associated with those responsibilities.

Varying the kinds of participation will result in more as well as better input. There will be less of a need for you to put yourself in "I have to do all the talking" mode, less of a need to pick on someone, and less chance of missing valuable contributions from quieter group members.

Strategy 5: Don't Mask the Task

"What is it we're supposed to be doing?" This is a question you should expect to hear because there will always be someone who does not understand the instructions, needs more information than what was initially provided, was distracted by something else or was simply not listening. There are a variety of ways you can set the attendees up for success.

Clearly communicate the parameters of the task. To minimize confusion and the need for repetition, ensure the instructions are also available on a presentation slide, a handout or an email. The simple act of preparing the instructions will clarify the assignment in your mind as well. The clearer you are in defining the task, the better the chances you will receive quality contributions. Everyone present will need to know the following:
- Objective of the assignment.
- Work group size—individual, pairs, triads, quads.
- Duration of the activity.
- Structure of the exercise.
- Expected deliverables.

Think of the objective and the deliverables as mirror images of each other. In order to get great ideas from your staff, you have to be clear on what you want from them. Notice the difference between the following objectives:
- List at least 3 departmental cost-cutting ideas

- Generate 3 cost-cutting ideas that will result in substantial savings to the department
- List 3 cost-cutting ideas that will each yield a minimum of $100,000 in savings to the department over the next fiscal year

The first two examples will yield less than adequate responses if what you are really looking for is the third outcome. The more specific you can be the better. Any possible misunderstandings or assumptions, along with preparation, research, discussion, decision-making and time spent on the task will vary depending on how clearly and specifically you articulate what you want. In my book, *Meeting with Success: Tips and Techniques for Great Meetings,* you will find detailed descriptions of a variety of effective techniques and activities for creative idea generation, brainstorming and problem solving.

Strategy 6: Make People Feel Safe

There are three types of safety that are key to getting the most participation from your employees at meetings: physical, emotional, and psychological. Let's assume that you already have a handle on physical safety. But have you given any thought to the other two types?

Emotional and psychological safety, or their lack, play out every day in the quantity and quality of employee engagement. Many employees hold themselves back from full participation at meetings for fear of rejection, of ridicule or even of losing their jobs. A safe environment allows them to take risks, to try out ideas and processes, or to offer up their suggestions without these fears. They feel free to be creative, spontaneous and even more importantly, to be themselves.

Safe is different from comfortable. Comfortable reminds me of a cozy quilt and a soft couch. If we never did anything that made us uncomfortable, we would never grow. The first time I rode a zip line, I was very uncomfortable—scared silly, in fact—but I put myself out there nonetheless. I had great instructors who taught me what I needed to know to be successful. With the right support, I was able to learn some new skills and enjoy the experience that day.

In my presentation skills workshops and coaching sessions I always push my clients outside their comfort zones, but I also give them the tools and the support they need. They are not left to flounder on their own.

There is a useful lesson in safety to be learned from an unlikely source—improvisational theater. What do improv and business meetings have in common? A lot! If you have ever watched or participated in improv, you may have been misled into thinking that it's all about comedy. Not so! Admittedly, comedy often surfaces as an enjoyable by-product of improv. What's key, though, is the collaboration around underlying communication principles that improvisers use and subscribe to as a foundation for creating a successful scene. These very same principles are applicable to a meeting environment.

One of these principles involves establishing a safe environment for both offering and accepting. Every "offer"—word, sentence, physical movement, facial expression—put forth by an improviser is accepted. No one ever reacts with, "That's stupid," or, "We've done that before and it didn't work," or, "No, we don't have budget for that." The improvisers observe their colleagues and then respond constructively. They may not like the offer they receive but they use it anyway as a foundation upon which they add on, modify, and develop the ideas until the desired end result is attained. How is that for creating a safe supportive environment?

Consider this as well: Many of the ideas presented by your staff may initially look like terrible ideas. Very few brilliant ideas are born brilliant. They begin as fragile thoughts that can easily be dismissed by an offhand remark or a negative comment. However, once they have been worked on, added to, chewed over and revised, they can often become earth-shatteringly good.

What are you doing to establish a safe environment that encourages your meeting attendees to offer up new ideas?

Strategy 7: Foster Creativity

When was the last time you were inspired by a meeting room? Many of them do nothing to stimulate the creative process. The walls are drab. There are no windows and the ventilation is poor. Yet employees attending meetings in these venues are expected to come up with clever, imaginative and innovative ideas.

Creativity often materializes when we least expect it, sometimes when we're engaged in an unrelated activity in an unrelated place. My clients tell me that they generate their best ideas while they are taking a shower, driving, running or listening to a motivational presentation.

If you want people to think outside the box, you have to take them outside the box. Consider a change of surroundings. Meet at an interesting restaurant, a golf course or outside on the back lawn of your office building. For a small group, conduct a walking meeting around the block or through a local park. Research published by Schaefer, et al (2010) in the *European Journal of Developmental Psychology* tells us that walking is good for the brain and the memory.

Consider providing visual aids and props at your meetings that stimulate ideas. These might include photos or samples of products from competitors or even from other types of businesses. Participants often draw inspiration from looking at how others do things.

If you cannot take your employees out of the box for meetings, there are ways that your organization can change the box to inspire and motivate them. At one of their software development facilities, IBM has four or five special-décor rooms. Each room has a theme such as a wilderness summer cottage or a South Seas beach cabin. To encourage cross-pollination of ideas, the software engineers are encouraged to lunch in these settings with members of other departments and project teams. What are you doing to foster creativity at your meetings?

Strategy 8: Use the "Yes, and" Principle to Move Ideas Forward

The meetings at the software company were showing some progress. There was an increase in both opinion-sharing and idea generation from some of the attendees, but according to the department manager something still seemed to be holding others back. A principle used in improvisational theater known as "Yes, and" may be helpful here.

Sometimes people are in a rush to have themselves heard and in their haste they ride roughshod over others' contributions. The "Yes, and" strategy helps people adopt a new way of responding to each other. "Yes, and" is about consciously picking up and using what is offered. "Yes" is the acknowledgement of someone's offer while "and" begins the response to it. The pattern then repeats, moving the conversation, idea or action along.

Think of it this way: In a game of football or basketball, everyone has their eye on the ball. No one ever ignores the person in possession of the ball because the players are eager to keep the play going. If someone does drop the ball, someone else is there to pick it up. This forward motion infuses the game with energy and fun. In a meeting, the "ball" is an idea. "Yes, and" keeps that ball in motion.

By the way, saying "Yes, and" does not necessarily mean that you agree with what the other person is saying. It is simply a way of affirming that you are listening and then constructively adding to, modifying or enhancing the idea. Agreeing to disagree still adheres to the "Yes, and" principle as long as the intention for both parties is to move forward.

Here is an example of how a conversation might unfold using this strategy. "Yes, and" has been placed in parentheses to indicate that the individuals may not actually verbalize these exact words, but the intent comes through in the conversation. The problem being dealt with is insufficient office space and the objective is to delay moving for two years.

Person A: Some employees might be willing to share their offices with a colleague.

Person 1: (Yes, and) some might want to work from home 2 or 3 days a week.

A: (Yes, and) they would save a lot of commuting time.

1: (Yes, and) they'd be able to spend more time with their families.

A: (Yes, and) they would also save on the cost of gas as well as the wear and tear on their cars.

1: (Yes, and) what about computer access?

A: (Yes, and) we could ask the IT department to arrange access to the database for those folks working from home.

1: (Yes and) I'm concerned that the remote workers will miss important meetings.

A: (Yes, and) we could schedule weekly conference calls with the entire team so everyone stays in the loop.

Using the "Yes, and" principle forces us to look for the value in every idea. It avoids shutting participants down and encourages growth. It creates an environment in which people feel empowered to pitch their ideas.

Strategy 9: Reward Them

Make certain that your attendees feel appreciated. Thank them for their time, efforts and contributions to the meeting. Be sure they know that they play an important part in reaching the objectives. Celebrate their project successes and important milestones.

Help them see the bigger picture, not just in their department, but also in other parts of the organization. Understanding how their responsibilities and contributions relate to other team members' jobs, the department and to overall corporate core values is critical. When they feel appreciated and see themselves as part of the team and the organization, they will be more engaged and take more ownership of the situation. That bodes well for future participation.

Strategy 10: Assess the Meeting

A project group at a pharmaceutical company was meeting once a month. Many of the attendees were bored with the long updates, which seemed irrelevant to their part of the project. One of the participants noted this and took the initiative in gaining approval from the meeting leader to distribute a meeting evaluation form to the other participants. Once the survey was completed and the results were tabulated, the facilitator and participants were able to suggest some action steps to remedy the issues raised in the survey. The results were shorter meetings that were more focused and productive, and which were only attended by representatives from the most applicable departments. Others were included in updates as needed.

Invite your group to evaluate its meeting management practices. Recognize that many of your staff will not openly provide feedback to you regarding your meeting. To encourage them to express their needs and any suggested changes constructively, while at the same time protecting the anonymity of the source, consider using an electronic survey. Also consider having an outside meeting facilitator conduct the evaluation on your behalf. The survey should ask questions about the use of meeting procedures, balance of input from attendees, clarity of responsibilities, managing differences of opinion, relevance of topics and so on. Share the results of the feedback with the group and then create action plans that will help put the changes into effect and set a new standard for effective meetings.

A Few Final Thoughts

Business wisdom tells us that principles and strategies mean nothing if they aren't put into action. The truth is that you really can make drastic changes to your meetings. Here, in summary, are the three key implementation strategies:

Engage others. When you involve others in thought, in conversation and in action, you can co-create a shared outcome that gains everyone's support, participation and enthusiasm.

Encourage others. Use the "Yes, and" principle to keep dialogue open. It is an essential tool for moving communication forward and stimulating others to be productive, creative and energized.

Empower others. By providing assistance and support, you can inspire others to take on the courage and confidence to succeed and grow. When you make others look good, you look good too.

I'll leave you with one last piece of wisdom from the world of improvisational theater: The key to successful meetings is being willing to observe what goes on around you, respond supportively to others and act constructively. What could be more applicable to business and life in general?

Appendix

TIGERS®
SUCCESS SERIES

Phone

Toll Free 1.877.538.2822
International 1.541.385.7465

Websites

Website: http://www.corevalues.com
Facebook: https://www.facebook.com/#!/TeamBuildingSuccess
LinkedIn: http://www.linkedin.com/in/diannecrampton
Twitter: https://twitter.com/Diannecrampton

- Complimentary Membership Program, Blog, Programs, Products, Services
- View a complimentary training on How To Build a Successful Work Environment Where Trust and Cooperation Thrive http://corevalues.com/how-to-build-a-successful-work-environment/

Book

TIGERS Among Us—Winning Business Team Cultures and Why They Thrive (Three Creeks, 2010) http://www.TigersAmongUs.com

Perfect Bound, E-book, and Quantity Discounts Available.

TIGERS Team Wheel Game™ & Facilitation Certification
http://www.corevalues.com/tigers-team-wheel-game

Master the use of our royalty-free catalytic tools and facilitation methods for team development and change planning. Our 3-Day Certification Retreats are offered twice a year. Turnkey and compatible with other team development resources.

Team Culture Survey

Measure the level of trust, interdependence, genuineness, empathy, risk and success within your organization to take the guesswork out of your workforce development goals. To experience a sample survey go to http://corevalues.com/tigers-team-survey/

Team Development Facilitation http://corevalues.com/team-wheel-group-facilitation/

From start to finish, an experienced TIGERS facilitator will guide your team to successfully identify and solve organizational issues in a one-day, two-day and three-day leadership retreats.

Mastering Team Consensus Building (Training)

This one-day training teaches internal and independent consultants, trainers and organizational development specialists to master the art of emotionally intelligent consensus facilitation. When high level commitment and accountability for decisions are desired outcomes, this program guides you step-by-step through a powerful process that engages every thinking and learning style. Hands-on, highly interactive and includes demonstration and practice. Self Study and On-Line programs are also available.

TIGERS Inner Circle Partnership

Join the Elite Inner Circle of TIGERS Certified Facilitators, Trainers, and Coaches to be recognized as a TIGERS® facilitator for potential referrals and partnering opportunities.

TIGERS Inner Circle Train the Trainer

Become a Certified TIGERS Facilitator and train other Facilitators. This is a unique partnership opportunity. Schedule a business call to learn more.

PEERLESS
LEADERSHIP DEVELOPMENT
Improved Productivity Through Better Relationships

Website:

http://www.PeerlessLeadership.com

Download your free report
"How to Establish Respect in the Workplace"

Contact:

Tony Lacertosa
31 Gorham Rd, #6402
Scarborough, ME 04070
207-883-1902
info@PeerlessLeadership.com

Services offered:

At Peerless Leadership Development, we are committed to seeing public and private organizations function more cohesively and improve their productivity through building better interpersonal relationships in the workplace. With that objective in mind, we can help you prevent or solve problems that you may have around:

- Building a culture of civility, respect and cooperation in your organization
- Dealing with difficult employees
- Training managers in how to have difficult conversations with employees
- Team building and development
- Collaborative leadership
- Developing action plans and gaining consensus for them among stakeholders
- Establishing productive, collaborative school-community partnership teams

For schools, in addition to all of the above, we also offer a student behavior management program that has been proven to reduce discipline problems by an average of 75% while improving academic performance and parental support.

More details about these services, which are custom designed for each organization, can be found on the website or by contacting Peerless Leadership Development.

Call 207-883-1902

or email

info@PeerlessLeadership.com

for more information about these programs.

A Couple of Activities

Ice breaking Activity—Behavior

An activity to get people talking to each other discovering who they are behaviorally. Every person will receive a package of 8 cards. There are 32 different cards to choose from. The goal is to trade cards to achieve the most accurate description of yourself.

• Maintains High Standards	• Seeks Power and Authority
• Diplomatic	• Positive, Likes Confrontation
• Critical Thinker	• Drives for Results
• Analytical and Precise	• Likes Challenging Assignments
• Organized	• Problem Solver
• Motivated by Accuracy	• Exhibits Strong Character
• Well Disciplined	• Talks with Hands
• Reserved	• Motivated by Directness
• Family Oriented	• Good at Persuading People
• Values Job Stability	• Socially and Verbally Aggressive
• Motivate by Standards	• High People Orientation
• Good Listener	• Team-Oriented
• Patient and Empathetic	• Facially Expressive
• Uses Limited Hand Gestures	• Very Optimistic
• Loyal to Those Who They Identify With	• Motivated by Recognition
• Like to Work in a Team Environment	• Can Communicate and See the Bigger Picture

Getting Started:

- 1-minute rounds, number of rounds dependent on size of class.
- You can only move to the next round after the 1-minute bell—use the time to trade and to get to know each other
- You do not have to trade cards to move to the next round
- You can trade as many cards as you like during each round
- You must both agree to the trade

For PowerPoint instruction slide set and template for 32 cards contact Info@viatechglobal.com Subject: Ice Breaker Card Activity.

Roles and Responsibilities

Here's a quick activity that can help clarify roles and responsibilities. Put flip-chart paper around the room. Have each individual go to their own flip-chart paper and write down what they see as their major roles and responsibilities, numbering each item. Then, have other team members wander around the room, adding and modifying others' charts. Then each individual returns to their own chart. Where they comment regarding their team member's additions

What do you agree with?	2&4
What do you disagree with?	5
What do you need clarified?	6

Facilitate a discussion until you agree on the majority of roles and responsibilities. This is simple stuff that brings a team together solving their problems.

For more information about Viatech Global
www.viatechglobal.com

Interested in Team Development workshops?
http://www.viatechglobal.com/services/team-development/

For information on our Train the Trainer program
http://www.viatechglobal.com/services/training-mentoring/

And information on our unique, assessment base selection program
http://www.viatechglobal.com/services/employee-selection/

For personalized service or additional information contact Michael Bouton 1 505-765-9903 or email at michael@viatechglobal.com

Viatech Global
28 Ridge Drive, Cedar Crest NM 87008
www.viatechglobal.com info@viatechglobal.com
1 505 765-9901 800 494-5218

Cornerstone Consulting International Resources

Phone

Toll Free (480) 664-9017

Website:

Http://www.CCSuccess.com

Email:

CCsuccess@q.com

Designing Job Rubrics Supplement

If you were interested in getting a better understanding of your staffing needs and want to understand how to utilize Job Rubrics in your company, you can me an email at CCSuccess@q.com, enter "*Job Rubric*" in the message line and I will send you the additional information to help improve your staffing process.

Thinking Style Assessment and Certification

Become a master at understanding how your Thinking affects your daily life. Take it one step further and understand how to work with others to help them understand how their thinking affects their decision, actions, and work with teams.

Executive Assessment and Leadership Team Training

Are you staffing a new executive position and what a more in depth understanding of what you will see on the job at 6 months or a year? Contact me about how to go about assessing all of your staffing needs. Do you need more from your team, but do not know how to get it? Have your team evaluated for strengths and limits and gain a new perspective for a positive and productive future.

TIGERS Certified Practitioner and Inner Circle Member

Explore the level of collaboration on both a team and company level. I will help your team to successfully identify and solve organizational issues in a one-day, two-day, or three-day leadership retreat. I can also help your company facilitate an emotionally intelligent consensus building program. When high level commitment and accountability for decisions are desired outcomes, this program guides you step-by-step through a powerful process that engages every thinking and learning style. Hands-on, highly interactive and includes demonstration and practice.

Ignite Your Relationships™ Business Resources

Business Consultation, Publicity & Marketing, Social Media, Networking, Conference & Seminar Events, and Book & Audio Product Publishing

Andrea Adams-Miller, MS, CHES, CEO & Founder
Keynote Speaker, Consultant, Trainer, Author, & Publisher

Mailing Address: PO BOX 443, Findlay, OH 45839

Phone: 1-419-722-6931

Email: Andrea@IgniteYourRelationships.com

Website: http://www.IgniteYourRelationships.com

Complimentary e-Newsletter Program, Sample Service Offerings through Video, e-Book, Teleseminars, Webinars, Blog Articles, & more...

Services & Programs*

- "Putting the Sizzle in Your Business 'REAL'ationships: Create, Retain, & Sustain Successful Real Relationships with Your Clients, Employees, Partners, & Vendors"
- "Healthy Relationships & Healthy Business Practices: Igniting the Spark, Fire, & Passion in Your Business, Organization, & Non Profit"
- "Social Media Revealed: Igniting the Spark, Fire, & Passion for Online Marketing Success"
- "Networking Secrets Revealed: Igniting the Spark, Fire, & Passion for Lucrative Success with New & Past Business Connections"
- "Books as Your Business Card: Igniting the Spark, Fire, & Passion for Lucrative Success with New Business Prospects"
- "Business Presentations that Wow!: Igniting the Spark, Fire, & Passion with Theater & Improvisational Skills to Keep Your Audience Captivated, Motivated, & Ready to Invest"

* Programs tailored to your business, conference, or event are available upon request. Each program has beginning, intermediate, and advanced learner modules/trainings.

Books by Andrea Adams-Miller*

- *Putting the Sizzle in Your Business 'REAL'ationships: The Ultimate Guide to Create, Retain, & Sustain Successful Real Relationships with Your Clients, Employees, Partners, & Vendors.* (2011). Avonlea Publishing Company; Ohio.
- *Healthy Relationships & Healthy Business Practices: Igniting the Spark, Fire, & Passion in Your Business, Organization, or Non Profit.* (2011). Avonlea Publishing Company; Ohio.
- *Social Media Revealed: Igniting the Spark, Fire, & Passion for Online Marketing Success.* (2012). Avonlea Publishing Company; Ohio.
- *Networking Secrets Revealed: Igniting the Spark, Fire, & Passion for Lucrative Success with New & Past Business Connections.* (2012). Avonlea Publishing Company; Ohio.
- *Books as Your Business Card: Igniting the Spark, Fire, & Passion for Lucrative Success with New Business Prospects.* (2012). Avonlea Publishing Company; Ohio.
- *Business Presentations that Wow!: Igniting the Spark, Fire, & Passion with Theater & Improvisational Skills to Keep Your Audience Captivated, Motivated, & Ready to Invest.* (2012). Avonlea Publishing Company; Ohio.

Books Co-Authored by Andrea Adams-Miller*

- *Jump-Start Your Success: The 23 Top Speakers Share Their Insights for Creating More Success, Wealth, & Happiness.* (2010) JMI, Inc.: United States.
- *Nothing But Net: The World's Leading Speakers, Trainers, & Entrepreneur's Reveal Their Top Secrets to Increase Your Bottom Line. (2012)* Celebrity Press™ Imprint: United States.

* Books available with quantity discount options at
http://www.IgniteYourRelationships.com

Kokott, Wood & Associates, LLC

Phone:
- Toll Free: 1.877.225.9789
- Atlanta: 678-935-1900
- Phoenix: 480-626-7540

Website:
- www.Kokott-Wood.com
- www.kokott-wood.blogspot.com

Company:

Kokott, Wood & Associates, LLC (KWA) was founded based on the principle of providing our customers—both clients and candidates—with executive search services done the right way. Keenly aware of the negative reputation the executive recruiting industry faces, we recognize the opportunities that a truly different and customer-centric approach creates. With extensive executive experience on both sides of the hiring equation, our unique and comprehensive process addresses the complex needs of the candidate and the hiring manager. As a result, we stand alone in our 100% placement rate.

Although originally focused on the downstream petroleum and convenience store marketing sectors, our approach to *hiring for fit* enables us to successfully place candidates at all levels in a wide variety of specialties such as:

• Retail—Operations, Marketing

• Sales—IT, OEM, CPG

• IT—Software Development, Project Management, DB Administration

• Logistics—Transportation, Warehouse

• Accounting

• Human Resources

• Training

We look forward to conducting your company's next executive search. With 80% of our business generated by repeat and referral customers, we're confident in our ability to exceed your expectations.

FOCUS YOUR BRILLIANCE!

Debra Zimmer

Contact

Phone: 720-878-6606

Email: deb@expertmarketingcoach.com

Web: http://ExpertMarketingCoach.com

Facebook: http://www.facebook.com/DebraZimmer

LinkedIn: http://www.linkedin.com/DebraZimmer

Twitter: http://www.twitter.com/DebraZimmer

Pinterest: http://www.pinterest.com/DebraZimmer

Mail: 98 Wadsworth Blvd., Ste. 127, PMB 115, Lakewood, CO 80226

Professional Services

- Social Media Strategy and Planning for Organizations, Executives, and Employees
- Social Media Training for Marketers, Executives and Employees
- Social Media Account Management
- Virtual Chief Marketing Officer consulting:
  - o Marketing Strategy
  - o Marketing Planning
  - o Marketing Team Building and Management

Handouts & Resources

Download handouts & reference materials for the chapter *"The Business Case for Social Media: 3 Ways to Engage Your Team and Grow Your Brand"* by registering at:

http://ExpertMarketingCoach.com/Gifts/ERG

Materials available here include:

- Articles and Reports
  - o 2012 CEO, Social Media & Leadership Survey by Brand Fog
  - o 2012 CEO.com Social CEO Report, by CEO.com
  - o The 2012 IBM CEO Study, *Leading Through Connections*
  - o Why Social Media Matters to Your Business, by Chadwick Martin Bailey
  - o The Social Divide—Employees, Executives Disagree on the Role of Social Media in Building Workplace Culture: Deloitte Survey
  - o Financial Post, "Executive tales from the Twitterverse: How ING Canada's CEO staked his brand on social media success," by Dan Ovsey
  - o "The $1.3 Trillion Price Of Not Tweeting At Work" Published on *Fast Company*
- How to Write Your Own Social Media Policy
  - o Social Media Policy Tool
  - o Directory of 200 Social Media Policy samples
  - o Social Media Policy Infographic
- Tutorials: "The 5 Secret Strategies to Social Media Success" video tutorial series
- Handouts: copies Michael Rapino Social Media Sites
- Infographics: data represented in a visual way

Dan Berryman is currently a Vice President
of Investments with JPMorgan Chase.

Dan also volunteers as a speaker for
civic organizations and offers complimentary
college business school seminars in Oregon.

Dan can be reached directly for questions at
(541) 601-1576.

For more information on the Objections Clinic, or to learn more about *conducting your own* Objections Clinic or *hosting* an Objections Clinic *on site* at your company, go to:

ObjectionsClinic.com

The Objections Clinic is an internet company owned and operated by Dan's wife, Kathleen.

Hurlburt Support Services Resources

"Strategies for Change

. . . the unexpected

and the desired."

Phone

1-907-240-6792

Website: Http://www.jhsupportservices.com

Custom Designed Trainings for Businesses:

"On Purpose" Training: Over time a company or individuals find it beneficial to reflect on or specifically address the purpose of the organization and the purpose for working there. This life-changing process is one of the most thought-provoking, empowering trainings available, This one-day training utilizes a cutting-edge format to engage participants in examining their individual purposes for work, and for the leaders to examine the purpose of the organization to see if it is still effective—all these beyond vision and mission statements and goals and objectives. 1 day with follow-up.

Systemic Change Development and Strategies: This training begins "where we are currently" to "where we want to be with all critical stakeholders onboard within defined timeframes." It utilizes a highly effective systemic change model based on the system-wide changes you want to implement. 2-4+ days with follow-up if desired

Strategies for Change for when "Life Happens:" Based on the changes that are impacting your work and are specific to your business for example personnel changes, together we will design a series of change processes that support your staff and provide leadership follow-up for key players. 1-2+ days with follow-up if desired

Trainer's Training: This training utilizes you and your staff's content expertise and experience. In it I will walk you through templates for designing and leading engaging, effective and long-lasting trainings with evaluation tools that will save your organization money and time. 1-2+ days with follow-up if desired

Talking about Time: This powerful training changes your thinking about how <u>structures</u> of time impact work and personal lives. It teaches several strategies for using structures of time to be more effective at work and in personal lives, while remaining "on purpose" toward goals. 1 to 2 days with follow-up if desired

Individual Business and Personal Coaching

Weekly or monthly coaching sessions on topics specific to your needs. Examples include but not limited to:
- Utilizing Time Structures
- Utilizing Purpose for work and life
- Clarifying what you want
- Exploring and conceiving possibilities
- Letting go of obstacles
- Determining and gathering resources
- Moving forward with congruence
- Nurturing growth and celebrating change
- Next steps

INTERNATIONAL, Inc.

Website: www.idashessel.com

Telephone: +1 (905) 882-5278

How Ida Shessel International, Inc. would like to be of service to you...

MEETING FACILITATION

http://idashessel.com/services/meeting-facilitation/

When you need an unbiased meeting leader to:
- engage the attendees in creative brainstorming, problem-solving, and decision-making
- empower everyone to participate, leveling the playing field between the diverse members of the group
- focus the meeting
- manage the process so you can participate

SPEAKING / WORKSHOPS

http://idashessel.com/services/speaking-workshops/

Your Best Presentation Ever
- learn how to give presentations that creatively engage your audience and achieve maximum impact

Business Memory Gym
- learn strategies that enhance sales results through better memory
- triple your memory and position yourself as a genius in your industry and business relationships
- adopt memory techniques developed by Dave Farrow, 2-time Guinness Record Holder for Greatest Memory

The Quick Communicator
- learn how to respond constructively to unexpected and unrehearsed situations in business
- enhance flexibility, creativity, speed, & collaboration in the workplace
- incorporate communication strategies drawn from the successful model used in improvisational theater & apply them to business situations

170

COACHING / CONSULTING

http://idashessel.com/services/coaching-consulting/

One-on-one attention for your regular or special-event meeting or presentation because you want:

- a specialist who can objectively identify your strengths and areas for improvement as a presenter
- a new source of creative ideas and strategies for your presentations from an expert
- someone to help you think through your meeting or presentation plan and ask the tough questions others won't ask

PRODUCTS http://idashessel.com/success-store/

Books, Action Guides, and Audio programs:

- *Communicate Like a Top Leader*

- *Meeting With Success*

- *Tip Booklets:*
  77 Tips for Absolutely Great Meetings

Free Special Reports www.idashessel.com